Tending the Soul

:: 90 days of spiritual nourishment ::

D1305096

CONTRIBUTIONS BY
SARA GROVES,
MARGARET FEINBERG,
JAN SILVIOUS
& MANY OTHERS

Tending the Soul

:: 90 days of spiritual nourishment ::

edited by the Women of Midday Connection:
Anita Lustrea, Melinda Schmidt & Lori Neff

MOODY PUBLISHERS
CHICAGO

Scripture quotations marked NASB are taken from the *New American Standard Bible®*, Copyright © 1960, 1962, 1963, 1968, 1971, 1972, 1973, 1975, 1977, 1995 by The Lockman Foundation. Used by permission. (www.Lockman.org)

Scripture quotations marked NIV are taken from the *Holy Bible, New International Version®*, NIV®. Copyright © 1973, 1978, 1984 by Biblica, Inc.™ Used by permission of Zondervan. All rights reserved worldwide.

Scripture quotations marked NLT are taken from the *Holy Bible, New Living Translation*, copyright © 1996, 2004. Used by permission of Tyndale House Publishers, Inc., Wheaton, Illinois 60189, U.S.A. All rights reserved.

Scripture quotations marked KJV are taken from the King James Version.

Scripture quotations marked NRSV are from the *New Revised Standard Version* of the Bible, copyright 1989, by the Division of Christian Education of the National Council of the Churches of Christ in the USA. Used by permission. All rights reserved.

Scripture quotations marked THE MESSAGE are from *The Message*, copyright © by Eugene H. Peterson 1993, 1994, 1995. Used by permission of NavPress Publishing Group.

Scripture quotations marked ESV are taken from *The Holy Bible, English Standard Version*. Copyright © 2000, 2001 by Crossway Bibles, a division of Good News Publishers. Used by permission. All rights reserved.

Scripture quotations marked NIRV are taken from the *New International Readers Version*. Copyright © 1996, 1998 Biblica. All rights reserved throughout the world. Used by permission of Biblica..

Scripture quotations marked HCSB are taken from the *Holman Christian Standard Bible®*, Copyright © 1999, 2000, 2002, 2003 by Holman Bible Publishers. Used by permission.

Scripture quotation marked PHILLIPS is from *The New Testament in Modern English by J.B. Phillips* © HarperCollins and J.B. Phillips 1958, 1960, 1972.

Library of Congress Cataloging-in-Publication Data

Tending the soul : 90 days of spiritual nourishment / edited by the women of Midday Connection—Anita Lustrea, Melinda Schmidt & Lori Neff.

   p. cm.

   ISBN 978-0-8024-1533-2

   1. Christian women—Prayers and devotions. I. Lustrea, Anita.

II. Schmidt, Melinda. III. Neff, Lori. IV. Midday connection (Radio program)

   BV4844.T4 2011

   242'.643—dc22

2010050645

Edited by Pam Pugh
Cover design: The Dugan Design Group

Interior Design: Rose DeBoer
Cover Image: Getty RF (#78399718)

We hope you enjoy this book from Moody Publishers. Our goal is to provide high-quality, thought-provoking books and products that connect truth to your real needs and challenges. For more information on other books and products written and produced from a biblical perspective, go to www.moodypublishers.com or write to:

Moody Publishers
820 N. LaSalle Boulevard
Chicago, IL 60610

1 3 5 7 9 10 8 6 4 2

Printed in the United States of America

:: CONTENTS ::

SECTION TWO

SECTION THREE

Friends Sharpening Friends

*W*omen need the voices of other women in their lives.

This is one reason we have compiled a second *Midday Connection* devotional. We read that "As iron sharpens iron, so a friend sharpens a friend" (Proverbs 27:17 NLT). We want to challenge and encourage one another to grow—spiritually, emotionally, intellectually, and physically. God cares about the whole person, and we've figured out that if we don't care for the whole person, we can remain broken and not able to fully walk into what God has for us as women.

In this 90-day devotional you'll encounter the voices of trusted friends. You'll hear the voices of the *Midday Connection* team and of some of our favorite guests from the last couple of years. You'll be pointed toward Scripture and enjoy a devotional thought wrapped up with a relevant prayer.

But we think the most important interaction with the book might be the time you spend in reflection. At the close of each selection, you'll find a question or thought starter for further consideration. You'll be asked to actively engage in the devotional in a way that may come easily to you—or may seem a bit of a stretch. As you reflect and open your heart to the spirit of God speaking gently to you, you're invited to:

- journal
- sketch
- compose a poem
- write a letter to God
- meditate on a hymn or worship song that comes to mind

Growing the whole person can't take place only in our mind; it has to happen in the whole of us. It's easy to "think" our way through our spiritual journey, but science tells us the more ways in which we can engage our senses, the more deeply we are able to live out what we have taken in. We hope that this devotional will help you to take these creative practices, which really are spiritual practices, into the rest of your life.

Tending our soul is a joy, it is work, it is coming to know our true selves and our Creator more deeply. It is the satisfaction of seeing growth that may surprise us but will always delight us!

> Warmly,
> Anita, Melinda, and Lori
> The *Midday Connection* Team

Tending the Soul

SECTION ONE

Inconvenient Circumstance?

:: ANITA LUSTREA ::

*A man named Lazarus was sick. He lived in Bethany
with his sisters, Mary and Martha. [Mary's] brother,
Lazarus, was sick. So the two sisters sent a message to
Jesus telling him, "Lord, your dear friend is very sick." . . .
So although Jesus loved Martha, Mary, and Lazarus,
he stayed where he was for the next two days.*

JOHN 11:1–3, 5–6 NLT

*L*ife circumstances are rarely convenient. God's idea
of good timing rarely lines up with mine. I remember
when I got a call from my mom that my dad had
collapsed on the patio of their home in Florida and was being
transported by ambulance to the hospital. She didn't know
why it happened and she didn't have enough information to
put my heart at ease. I was helpless to do anything except
wait.

Mary and Martha sent word for Jesus to come, but He
didn't. I'm sure they waited in expectation of His coming. But
Jesus didn't come, and Lazarus died. God, in the flesh, was
nearby and He chose not to preempt His friend's death. Jesus

had another plan in mind. He would display His power like never before. He would raise Lazarus from the dead.

As Jesus finally turned toward Bethany, Martha got word He was on His way and went to meet Him. Scripture says, "But Mary stayed in the house." I think Mary remained behind because she was hopping mad at Jesus for not dropping everything and coming to her brother's rescue, to her rescue. Once we turn our lives over to Christ, we enter a new playing field, one where we cannot predict the outcome, but where we can trust the character of the one at the helm.

Rarely do we have a view of why circumstances occur . . . why my dad needed open-heart surgery, for example. We can trust our good God to work every situation for our good, even if it appears He's lingering somewhere else for a few extra days.

> *Lord, help me trust You even when Your timing*
> *doesn't line up with mine. Give me vision to see*
> *Your goodness even in the middle of the mess.*
> *Amen.*

REFLECTION: Look back on a difficult circumstance. What aspects of God's character can you now see because of hindsight? How might that encourage you for the future?

Journal, sketch, compose a poem, write a letter to God,
meditate on a hymn or worship song that comes to mind.

Delight

:: CHRISTINE WYRTZEN ::

I will delight in your statutes;
I will not forget your word.

PSALM 119:16 ESV

*M*any days, when cross-referencing from one passage to another, I discover a tie-in between stories I never knew were related. It is so cool! I will talk about it for weeks. It's easy to delight in God's statutes on those occasions.

What about days when I'm prone to worry? Do I delight in His words that address my fear? When I'm depressed over my mistakes, do I take joy in His words that remind me of His mercy? When I'm nursing a grudge, do I love His words about forgiveness? I can easily live like a child who loves commandments that are naturally appealing but despise ones that tell me to do something I don't want to do.

Every single day brings a set of circumstances that challenge my love for God's ways. I will not instinctively love His Word when it corrects me, when it causes me to stretch beyond what's comfortable, when it beckons me to move out of a familiar set of emotions that aren't good for me. They may be as comfortable as my favorite old shirt and pair of jeans but the outfit is really a set of grave clothes. Jesus' call is to come out of the tomb into resurrection life. That sounds inspirational and appealing until I find how resistant I am to the Light. I prefer, many times, to live in my tomb. The ways of the flesh are the ways of death. I know this, yet they're just so ingrained in this fallen nature. I must tell myself, many times a day, to embrace the ways of God.

David's promise to delight in God's statutes is really two things—it is a sentimental expression, and it is an expression of commitment.

> *Heavenly Father, I know myself well. I will forget if I*
> *don't vow to delight. Sometimes I will feel like it and*
> *just embrace You without a thought. Other times, I*
> *will need Your grace. Help me, Lord, at all points*
> *today. Amen.*

REFLECTION: What area in my life feels the riskiest to trust God today? Am I willing to stand on a new promise that reveals the opposite of how I feel? God, help me!

Journal, sketch, compose a poem, write a letter to God,
meditate on a hymn or worship song that comes to mind.

Keep Paddling!

:: PAM FARREL ::

Be steadfast.
1 CORINTHIANS 15:58 NASB

I love kayaking. The fresh air, warmth of the sun, the splash of the water, and the adventure draw me into a God-woman conversation. When my book *Woman of Confidence: Step into God's Adventure for Your Life* was released, I wanted to celebrate with an adventure. I gathered my "seasoned sisters" (friends over forty), and together we headed to beautiful Echo Ranch on Berner's Bay outside Juneau, Alaska. My friend Debbie, an experienced adventurer who has headed up numerous mission trips worldwide and is an award-winning outdoor educator, trained this all-girl cadre with safety tips.

I also learned much for life from Debbie's wisdom. There is a 50/50 rule in Alaska: if you are 50 feet from shore and fall into frigid water, you have a 50/50 chance of making it out alive. Training is vital to safety! Often in life, God places training reminders of His truth along life's journey.

One morning, we set out on glassy water but the wind picked up, causing whitecaps. Debbie spoke courage into our hearts that I continue to carry with me as it echoes God's approach to handle the storms. She advised, "Face it head-on. Aim your bow directly into the wave."

God tells us, "Press on toward the goal for the prize of the upward call of God" (Philippians 3:14 NASB). *Dig deep. Push hard. Aim for the shore. It may hurt, but you can do this.*

And, "For momentary, light affliction is producing for us an eternal weight of glory" (2 Corinthians 4:17 NASB). *Keep paddling. Paddling is your stability.*

Remember what He says: "But you must keep your faith steady and firm. Don't move away from the hope that the good news holds out to you" (Colossians 1:23 NIRV).

> *Lord, give me power to paddle through the waves of my storm! Amen.*

REFLECTION: Mary Slessor, who as a single woman missionary paddled deep into the African jungle alone to take the gospel, had a line scribbled in the margin of her Bible, "God and one are a majority." With God's help, where does He want you to "keep paddling"? With God's help, how can you navigate the waves head-on?

Journal, sketch, compose a poem, write a letter to God, meditate on a hymn or worship song that comes to mind.

Faithful Love "In Spite Of"

:: NICOLE BRADDOCK BROMLEY ::

> *Many claim to have unfailing love,*
> *but a faithful person who can find?*
>
> PROVERBS 20:6 NIV

We come to understand the importance of our faithfulness to others when we ourselves experience the bitterness of betrayal.

Relationships should be a two-way street with reciprocal care and kindness, but when hurts and misunderstandings come into play, it becomes easy to disregard faithfulness. Wounding words and actions make it difficult to love faithfully, but they don't give us a right to react unlovingly.

God calls us to a higher road in relationship—to be His hands, feet, and mouthpiece to the world. Yet, when we are mistreated, our inclination is to fight back with gossip or judgment, or to simply jump ship. This comes from a false assumption that love requires a return; but when Jesus is our example, we know that real love and faithfulness will love others even when we are not loved back.

This doesn't mean we have to be there for everyone at all times. It doesn't mean we are to be a doormat to those who will take advantage of us. It does mean, however, that we are to be loving in the way we speak of one another and be faithful in prayer (Ephesians 4:29), even if that's from a distance. We will all fail one another at some point; not one of us is completely faithful or trustworthy. Only one man held true to those characteristics: Jesus. And only through Him can we be declared righteous.

If the question posed in Proverbs 20:6 is speaking to us today, then we should strive to love more faithfully. Never forget that you've received mercy and undeserved forgiveness. When you have a choice between spewing judgment and bitterness or extending mercy and love, I challenge you to let love and mercy win.

> *Father, I submit to You my relationships and the hurts that go along with them. I acknowledge that You redeem, restore, and reward those who earnestly seek You and live out Your commands. Help me to love the way You love me, forgive as You have forgiven me, and to be faithful as You are so faithful to me.*

REFLECTION: As a reflection of God's faithfulness to us, to whom is God asking you to reach out with the same faithfulness and love?

Journal, sketch, compose a poem, write a letter to God, meditate on a hymn or worship song that comes to mind.

Envying the Arrogant

:: SARA GROVES ::

They have no struggles;
their bodies are healthy and strong.
They are free from the burdens common to man.

PSALM 73:4–5 NIV

'm partial to this psalm because I lived out this very conversation with God. My heart had been growing cold, and I was up to no good. A natural rule follower, I was exhausted from trying to do everything right, and began to blame God for my troubles. I felt like I was bearing the weight of the moral universe somehow, and wanted to live carefree, without regard for some great battle between good and evil. I envied my neighbors who seemed to live for themselves without apology, and wondered why I tried so hard to be "good."

"If I had said, 'I will speak thus,' I would have betrayed your children." The psalmist Asaph starts to wake up in verse 15, as he asks God to please explain why those who disregard God's commands seem so happy. I wish I could see with my own eyes what God reveals to him in the next few verses, but in the ancient biblical text he conveys the revelation: wicked men are swept away like a bad dream. There is nothing built, nothing grown, nothing eternal in the life lived for self.

In contrition, Asaph realizes that external circumstances, wealth, health, fame, and so on are no reflection of what is real and eternal.

The most meaningful part of this psalm, and of my own story comes next. Here Asaph has been "senseless and igno-rant . . . a brute beast before you." But almost in surprise, he continues, "Yet, I am always with you; you hold me by my right hand" (vv. 22–23). God does not abandon us to our hard questions, but reveals Himself, and His love for us instead.

Asaph and I cry in unison, "Whom have I in heaven but you? And earth has nothing I desire besides you. My flesh and my heart may fail, but God is the strength of my heart and my portion forever . . . it is good to be near God."

> *Lord, thank You for hearing me out when I was*
> *senseless and selfish. Thank You for showing me*
> *how Your precepts are lifegiving, and are for my*
> *good!*

REFLECTION: Have you ever "envied the arrogant"? Do God's rules feel oppressive, or life-giving?

Journal, sketch, compose a poem, write a letter to God,
meditate on a hymn or worship song that comes to mind.

Peace in the Challenge

:: LAURA HENDRICKSON ::

God is the blessed controller of all things.
1 TIMOTHY 6:15 PHILLIPS

*M*y son Eric was diagnosed with autism when he was a toddler. After a year in a very intensive early intervention program at a clinic at UCLA, we returned home, where I was expected to direct his ongoing training. I was overwhelmed by this responsibility! The consequences of failure were so serious that I exhausted myself trying to manage every detail perfectly.

One evening, after spending hours trying to teach a difficult task to an uncooperative four-year-old, I collapsed on my bed in tears. Eric's future was at stake, and I thought it would be my fault if he didn't develop to his full potential. The responsibility was too great for me to bear! How could I ensure that he'd learn everything he needed to know? Full of fear, I cried out to the Lord.

He met me in a powerful way, showing me that in trying to bear this crushing burden alone, I was behaving as if I had no

God. I was burning myself out, relying on myself instead of Him. He didn't give up on me, but continued to direct the circumstances of our lives for good. What a relief! I realized that He's committed to us, loves us, and is in control of everything.

Today Eric's a man, and it's even more obvious than when he was a toddler that I can't control what happens to him. But the Lord can. Although sometimes I still forget to look to Him in faith, He's always faithful to Eric and me. He's just that good to His beloved children!

> *Gracious Father, my responsibilities overwhelm me when I forget that You're in control, and live as though it's all up to me. Thank You that You always forgive me when I fail to see Your loving hand guiding, directing, and caring for me, and try to do life on my own. I'm so grateful for Your faithfulness to me! Please give me the grace to look to You in faith through every challenge I'll encounter today.*

REFLECTION: Find some art books or pictures online that portray a restful scene. Pray the prayer above and know this is where God wants to lead you today.

Journal, sketch, compose a poem, write a letter to God, meditate on a hymn or worship song that comes to mind.

Trusting God with Our Burdens

:: ARLOA SUTTER ::

When I consider your heavens, the work of your fingers,
the moon and the stars, which you have set in place,
what is man that you are mindful of him?

PSALM 8:3–4 NIV

eing in nature gets us in touch with God's immense power and greatness. The sky filled with stars at night, ocean waves crashing, magnificent mountain peaks, wildflowers scattered over a meadow. All these and more reflect God's creative wonder and extravagant attention to detail.

While backpacking on the Appalachian Trail in North Carolina, I was intrigued by the mushrooms I saw along the path. I learned there are more than 14,000 different species of mushrooms. God could have created one kind of flower, or perhaps two or three, and the world would have been beautiful. But there are over 30,000 identified species of orchids alone! There is effusiveness to God's character, an overflowing extravagance. In his book *City of God*, Saint Augustine called it the "plentitude" of God, as the lavish, overflowing love and creativity of God is bountifully displayed in nature.

Like the psalmist who was awestruck at the beauty of the sky at night, the grandeur of God's creation leads us to wonder, "Who am I that you care about me?" The God who takes the time to design and maintain a garden of more than 30,000 species of orchids has all the resources needed to look after you. You are created with intimate care and precision. Every detail of your life was known by God before you were even born. "All the days ordained for me were written in your book before one of them came to be" (Psalm 139:16 NIV).

You can rest today in the truth that God loves you and cares about the details of your life. God is big enough and resourceful enough to meet your needs.

> *Lord, though I often feel weak and insignificant, I know You love me and will take care of me as You do all of Your creation. As I consider the birds and the flowers You have made and I see how bountifully You meet their needs, I am assured that the biggest challenge I face today is nothing for You to handle. I trust myself to Your extravagant care.*

REFLECTION: What challenge do you face today that you need to entrust to your Creator? Ask God to show you one way to off-load your burden onto Him today.

Journal, sketch, compose a poem, write a letter to God, meditate on a hymn or worship song that comes to mind.

The Importance of Compañeros

:: MELINDA SCHMIDT ::

*Then some women from our group of his
followers were at his tomb early this morning,
and they came back with an amazing report.*

LUKE 24:22 NLT

*I*n a rather odd scenario in Luke 24, two of Jesus' followers find themselves joined by a fellow traveler, who is, in fact, Jesus Himself—but unrecognized by them. These men sadly recount to this stranger the facts of Jesus' ministry and their disappointment that their supposed Messiah was crucified, and their hopes right along with Him.

As they earnestly discuss what's happened, they tell of a group of women—Mary Magdalene, Joanna (the wife of Herod's business manager), Mary, the mother of James, Salome, and several other unnamed women—who have just found Jesus' empty tomb that very morning. These women, they say, were "from our group."

"From our group." There was a space for women in Jesus' band of followers. These were kindred spirits who broke ranks with their corrupted religion and began to follow a prophet who healed people's bodies and their souls, despised inauthentic faith, and called them out to leave convention behind and follow Him into an unknown spiritual apprenticeship.

In her book *Pilgrimage of a Soul*, Phileena Heuertz speaks of our longing for *compañeros*, Spanish for "companions." As Christ-followers on a journey, "there are times when we feel we can't go on. We grow weary, we are injured along the way, our hope wavers." We long for *compañeros*—companions—to experience life with Christ alongside us.

The women who found Jesus' empty tomb were our spiritual ancestors, women who, along with their male counterparts such as Peter, Matthew, Lazarus, and Cleopas, were doing this new kind of spiritual journey together.

> *Jesus, please help me to find other women who will be my compañeros as I seek to follow You. Help me to sense when I have a wise woman in my presence. Teach me to seek out the wisdom of different generations of women, both younger and older.*

REFLECTION: Who are the companions with whom you can relate spiritually? Are you looking for them? Write a prayer and tell Jesus about your need for spiritually interested women who will do life with you. Commit to pray that prayer for as long as it takes to welcome them.

Journal, sketch, compose a poem, write a letter to God, meditate on a hymn or worship song that comes to mind.

The Attentive Savior

:: LISA HARPER ::

Soon afterward, Jesus went to a town called Nain,
and his disciples and a large crowd went along with
him. As he approached the town gate, a dead person
was being carried out—the only son of his mother,
and she was a widow. And a large crowd
from the town was with her.

LUKE 7:11–12 NIV

This poor woman is doubly grieved because she's lost her husband and her only son—which means she's facing emotional and financial destitution because she has no one left to care for her. She's not worrying about having to eat Ramen noodles or the pending mortgage payment right now. Instead she's weeping with uncontrollable grief as she trudges alongside the pallbearers who are carrying her boy out of town in an open casket. She doesn't even notice the gentle stranger who stops to stare at their sad parade.

That's why what happens next is so moving. The wailing widow doesn't ask for a miracle—Luke's narrative implies she doesn't even know who Jesus is—yet He compassionately crashes the funeral procession and grants one anyway.

"When the Lord saw her, his heart went out to her and he said, 'Don't cry.' Then he went up and touched the coffin . . . (and) said, 'Young man, I say to you, get up!' The dead man sat up and began to talk, and Jesus gave him back to his mother" (Luke 7:13–15 NIV).

Can you imagine that mama's expression? I bet her eyes were as big as saucers and she quickly grabbed her resurrected son in an enthusiastic bear hug. She probably didn't let go until he finally squeaked, "Mom, I can't breathe" in gentle protest!

Regardless of the particulars of your personal story—whether you've been blessed to be an actual mother or you're childless like me and borrow your friends' offspring when you need a kid-fix—it does every woman good to remember our Savior is wildly attentive to our needs. He knows and cares about the details of our lives. Even when we don't recognize His nearness, Jesus is still Immanuel . . . *God with us.*

> *Dear Jesus, thank You for Your consistent presence*
> *and compassion in every single moment of our*
> *lives. Amen.*

REFLECTION: Read Psalm 139. Write about the ways God has demonstrated His nearness to you during a recent difficult season.

Journal, sketch, compose a poem, write a letter to God,
meditate on a hymn or worship song that comes to mind.

Transforming Marital Intimacy

:: LINDA DILLOW ::

Let your fountain be blessed, and rejoice in the wife of your youth. As a loving hind and a graceful doe, let her breasts satisfy you at all times; be exhilarated always with her love.

PROVERBS 5:18–19 NASB

What do you see in these verses? I see pleasure. I see delight. I see fun. I see freedom, abandonment, intoxication, ecstasy.

What do these words say to me as a wife? I am to be a flowing fountain of pleasure for my husband. I am to be a loving doe, a graceful deer; so cute, so soft that my husband wants to reach out and cuddle me. And there's more.

God's Word encourages my husband and yours to:

Let his wife's breasts satisfy him always, and

Be captivated, exhilarated, intoxicated always with her physical love.

This straightforward passage doesn't leave much to the imagination, does it? It seems very strong. But it is God's Word and encourages me that as a wife, I am to be a delightful source of refreshing pleasure to this husband I love. I am to intoxicate him with my physical love—always. That means every year of our marriage. Of course, all that I am to be and do goes for him, too. He is to intoxicate me as well. Amen and amen.

Claire couldn't say "Amen" to God's view of intimacy. From a young age, she had been sexually abused and the idea of sex made her sick. Every area of her marriage to her best friend was wonderful except . . . you know what. Claire made a choice to bathe herself in God's Word and asked Him to re-fashion her mind. Recently when she read her story in *What's It Like to Be Married to Me?* she called me and shouted over the phone: "I am not that woman anymore!"

God's Spirit and God's Word totally refashioned Claire. Today she can say Amen to intoxicating intimacy with her lover and best friend. The Healer loves to transform His precious women. Will you pray this dangerous prayer?

> *My Father, reshape my heart and mind until it looks like YOUR perspective on sexual intimacy.*

REFLECTION: What is it like to make love with me?

Journal, sketch, compose a poem, write a letter to God, meditate on a hymn or worship song that comes to mind.

A Chance to Trust

:: KRISTEN ANDERSON ::

May the God of hope fill you with all joy and peace
as you trust in him, so that you may overflow
with hope by the power of the Holy Spirit.

ROMANS 15:13 NIV

When I was seventeen years old, I attempted suicide by lying on a set of train tracks. I was run over by thirty-three freight train cars moving along at 55 miles per hour. I lost both of my legs that night.

I had been through some rough times, including losing three of my friends and my grandmother in the two years prior . . . and I'd been raped. I had never ever thought that I would get to the point of trying to end my life, but I didn't think I could deal with the pain anymore. I felt hopeless. I never dreamed I could *overflow* with hope!

A small part inside of me knew that finding hope was possible, but I had no idea how to get from point A to point B. I'm thankful God gave me another chance to live and to learn. After my survival, I accepted Jesus, and He brought me hope and so much more. Romans 15:13 explains that God can overflow us with hope, and fill us with joy and peace. However, we must do our part in receiving these gifts by continually putting our trust in Him.

I used to put my trust in my family, my friends, and my possessions, but they were bound to let me down. When I began to trust God with everything . . . *everything*—started to change! God took my broken, empty, and hopeless heart and filled it until hope spilled out. Yes, bad things still happen, but now I know where to turn. No matter who you are, you can always trust God, and by the power of the Holy Spirit, He will fill your heart and your life with His hope, His peace, and His joy . . . just as He continues to fill mine.

> *Dear God, I pray that You would help me learn how to put my trust in You. I know that anything else I put my trust in will eventually fail me. Please, draw me closer to You and Your Son, Jesus. I want to accept and experience the gifts of hope, peace, and joy that You have for me.*

REFLECTION: In what area of your life do you need to trust God above all else?

Journal, sketch, compose a poem, write a letter to God, meditate on a hymn or worship song that comes to mind.

Leaps of Faith

:: CAROL RUHTER AND MARTY RAMEY ::

"Come," he said. Then Peter got down out of the boat,
walked on the water and came toward Jesus.

MATTHEW 14:29 NIV

Wood ducklings are small enough to fit into a teacup. But their leap of faith is huge.

Unlike most ducks that nest along lakes and rivers, colorful wood ducks choose to nest high in tree cavities or man-made nest boxes. In spring, the female lines the new home with wood chips and down from her breast and lays six to fifteen tan eggs; 80 percent will hatch. Thirty days after incubation, the first shell begins to crack; by day's end, down-covered ducklings fill the nest.

Then comes the call. Within twenty-four hours after the ducklings hatch, their mama checks for predators and then calls the hatchlings to join her far below the nest. By jumping. Even though the ducklings cannot yet fly, they must abandon the nest to reach wetland food below. They can plunge twenty feet and land unhurt—or up to an amazing 290 feet. Sometimes their nest towers over water, making for a softer landing; sometimes not.

So, these one-day-old puffballs teeter at the nest opening. If they don't leap, they'll starve. If they wait too long, their mother will be gone.

Ever teeter at the edge of a safe nest, listening to Jesus call . . . hungering for Him, but afraid to take the plunge? Take a lesson from hatchlings. The only thing you need to know in leaps of faith is who you're leaping toward.

> *I love You, Creator of all creatures great and small. I want to walk with You, wherever You lead. Fill me with a hunger for You, discernment to follow Your voice, and courage to come where You call. Lord, help me to know that no matter how far I leap in faith, Your arms and love are great enough to catch me. Amen.*

REFLECTION: Will you come when He calls? To what is He calling you? Do you find yourself resisting? Why?

Journal, sketch, compose a poem, write a letter to God, meditate on a hymn or worship song that comes to mind.

Breathtaking, Magnificent Creator

:: TRACEY BIANCHI ::

*The heavens declare the glory of God; the skies proclaim
the work of his hands. Day after day they pour forth
speech; night after night they display knowledge. There
is no speech or language where their voice is not heard.*

PSALM 19:1–3 NIV

Most of us spend a significant amount of our time indoors. Whether at home or work, school or the grocery store, the design of our contemporary lives keeps us mostly sheltered inside, even in some of the more generous climates.

And while of course this is often time well spent, we can struggle to understand the goodness of God as seen through His creation because of our inside lives. We just cannot grasp the glory of God inside the mall or a movie theater the way we might in an open field on a starry night.

When I slip outside on a summer evening to see the heavens declaring the glory of God, I can watch the clouds take their final forms of the day. They soften to a crimson glow as night slowly overtakes. Then God's stars begin to shimmer and poke holes in the looming, deep blue night. And, I wonder if the apostles Paul or James or Jesus Himself once gazed upon that same star.

When my tired body rallies itself before sunrise, I watch the soft purple, predawn sky yield to bursts of morning light, and I am reminded of Psalm 118, that this is indeed the day that the Lord has made, and there is much to rejoice and be glad in. This reminder is breathtaking, magnificent, and it shapes my soul because I dared to step outside and see God proclaiming His handiwork in the very sky that hovers over my head.

In the busy, inside nature of our lives, let us take time to marvel at God and His creative wonders that proclaim the works of His hands each and every day. Let us find encouragement and grace in the beautiful picture God has painted for us.

> *Lord, help me see Your love and grace in the creation all around me. Help me know Your presence through the beautiful world You have created.*

REFLECTION: Where do you see God's glory and magnificence displayed before you today? Check out Louie Giglio's "Laminin" clip on YouTube about the glory of God in creation.

Journal, sketch, compose a poem, write a letter to God, meditate on a hymn or worship song that comes to mind.

Can Anything Good Come of My Brokenness?

:: MIRIAM NEFF ::

But Ruth replied, "Don't urge me to leave you or to turn back from you. Where you go I will go, and where you stay I will stay. Your people will be my people and your God my God. Where you die I will die, and there I will be buried. May the Lord deal with me, be it ever so severely, if anything but death separates you and me."

RUTH 1:16–17 NIV

The road to Bethlehem was hard for Jesus' mother, Mary. Another woman traveled that same road. Ruth, the widow, the Moabite, *chose* to travel that tough road. Out of tragedy, losing her husband, father-in-law, and brother-in-law, she chose to become an immigrant. She turned her back on her culture, roots, family, religious cult, and chose to be *transformed*. She left the known for the unknown. She turned from a god that demanded infant sacrifice to the true God who treasures life.

The walk and witness of another widow, her mother-in-law, Naomi, won Ruth's heart, her head, and became the Bible Ruth *read* to become a believer. Ruth watched Naomi cling to her God in spite of losing all that women of that day treasured.

Ruth's words of commitment are often quoted in wedding ceremonies. But they resulted from two broken widows struggling to move on to a better life.

Even when Naomi's grief clouded her thinking, coloring her feelings bitter though she was blessed with a loyal daughter-in-law, Ruth still listened. She trusted her judgment, followed her instructions, and provided for her with hard work. Ruth knew Naomi had her best interests in her heart. The result: God blessed them both!

Do you wonder if anything good can come of your tragedy? Are you afraid to speak honestly of your loss? Are you afraid to talk about God?

Remember Ruth watched a real woman, and was converted on the road to Bethlehem.

> *Lord, help me be real, transparent, and trusting on*
> *my hard road. Give me courage when I can't see*
> *how this journey will end.*

REFLECTION: How is Jesus walking with you, holding your hand, or carrying you on *your* road to Bethlehem?

Journal, sketch, compose a poem, write a letter to God,
meditate on a hymn or worship song that comes to mind.

Longing for Quiet

:: NANCY KANE ::

Cease striving and know that I am God.
PSALM 46:10 NASB

*T*t is the disease of our age, CPAS—Continuous Partial Attention Syndrome, a term coined by Linda Stone, a former Microsoft executive. Continuous Partial Attention is multitasking on steroids. It is when you are on your cell phone or BlackBerry while also typing on your computer, listening to music, and at the same time answering a question from your child or other important person. It is multitasking throughout the day, continuously devoting only partial attention to each act or person you encounter. It is a state of always being on, never at rest, hypervigilant to everything around us. "We pay continuous partial attention in an effort *not to miss anything*," explains Stone. "It is an always-on, anywhere, anytime, anyplace behavior that involves an artificial sense of constant crisis." Between ever-ringing cell phones, beeping texts, alerts from our e-mails, we are easily distracted and can slowly lose a clear focus of our lives.

Yet, we instinctively know we were meant for something more. We long for the quiet moments when life slows down long enough to appreciate the beauty of a bright clear morning or hear the laughter of a child at play. We long too for moments to be known and loved.

God tenderly whispers His invitation to move apart from the frenetic pace to something richer and ultimately more meaningful that addresses our deepest longings—for intimacy and rest with Him. He can be trusted to do what we can never do for ourselves. If we allow Him, He can guide us to the quiet streams of water to rest, be renewed, and to focus our attention to one thing—to allow Him to love us and to love Him more deeply. Jesus' invitation is clear. "Come to me, all of you who are weary and carry heavy burdens, and I will give you rest" (Matthew 11:28 NLT).

Lord, be my tender companion today. Form and shape this day in such a way that I live my life in close connection with You and fulfill what You have called me to do. In all things today may my heart's affection be only of pleasing and loving You.

REFLECTION: What is it that has captured your attention and keeps you from quietly resting in God's presence?

Journal, sketch, compose a poem, write a letter to God, meditate on a hymn or worship song that comes to mind.

In the Presence

:: SANDRA WILSON ::

*O Lord, my heart is not lifted up; my eyes are not
raised too high; I do not occupy myself with things too
great and too marvelous for me. But I have calmed and
quieted my soul, like a weaned child with its mother;
like a weaned child is my soul within me. O Israel,
hope in the Lord from this time forth and forevermore.*

PSALM 131 ESV

*H*as a Scripture passage you know you've read before
ever leaped out at you as though for the first time?
This was my recent experience with Psalm 131. And
its unusual imagery challenged and changed my prayer life.

The psalmist begins by declaring that he does not come
before God with a proud heart or a presumptuous mind de-
manding answers to all of life's difficult questions. Many are
just "too great" to comprehend.

Then using maternal imagery to portray his relationship
with God in verse 2, the psalmist describes what he *does* do.
He comes to God like a "weaned child." That term may sound
strange to us, but it is significant enough for the psalmist to
repeat. He knows that an unweaned child comes to the
mother with an agenda: milk. And that's appropriate. But an

older, weaned child comes to the loved parent simply to be near her, having learned to trust the mother's nurturing care enough to surrender agendas and rest calmly in her presence.

God repeatedly invites us to bring our concerns and requests to Him in prayer. Yet if that pattern monopolizes our personal worship, we won't know the delight of relinquishing our agendas and coming to God solely because God is worth our complete attention. Try taking some prayer time to silently focus your heart and mind on our Savior God. Ask for nothing. Simply rest in His presence.

Psalm 131 ends with an exhortation to "hope in the Lord." When we learn to delight in God's *presence*—even more than in God's *presents*—He becomes the source and object of our hope. And we discover the peace of a weaned child.

> *Loving Lord, teach me to seek You more than what I want from You, to hope in You more than in what You provide. Amen.*

REFLECTION: What do you seek to calm and quiet your soul; in what or whom do you hope?

Journal, sketch, compose a poem, write a letter to God, meditate on a hymn or worship song that comes to mind.

Name Tag

:: MARGARET FEINBERG ::

*But whoever did want him, who believed he was who
he claimed and would do what he said, He made to be
their true selves, their child-of-God selves.*

JOHN 1:12 THE MESSAGE

*T*recently attended a gathering in which everyone wore
badges that identified their name, company, and hometown. Without the badge, you weren't allowed to enter.
For the first few days, I found myself skimming past the
names of the people I encountered and focusing on their company. From this small tag, I could pigeonhole them into their
purpose for attending, and even make assumptions about
their professional role and background.

All from a name tag.

Over the course of the week, I met with many of these tag
wearers, and what I discovered over a cup of coffee or meal
was so far beyond what those badges could communicate.
One woman had been battling the pain and exhaustion of fi-
bromyalgia for more than two years. Another longed to quit

her job, but had nowhere to go. One was still trying to complete a degree. Another regretted never earning one.

None of these stories were on the name tags. Finding out such meaningful details required going beyond a person's name and into their lives.

I sometimes wonder what name tag we'll be wearing in the banquet halls of heaven—the marriage supper of the Lamb. How will we be identified? What will our tag say?

In the gospel of John, Eugene Peterson in *The Message* eloquently writes of Christ, "But whoever did want him, who believed he was who he claimed and would do what he said, He made to be their true selves, their child-of-God selves."

In my mind's eye, I can see God removing our earthly tags so He can allow our true identities to shine through. In the true self, the child-of-God self the Scripture describes, I am empowered to becoming something greater than myself, namely, Christlike. And that is the greatest tag I will ever wear.

> *Oh God, help me claim my true identity so I can live powerfully for You. Amen.*

REFLECTION: What adjectives would you use to describe yourself, your true identity, as a child of God?

Journal, sketch, compose a poem, write a letter to God, meditate on a hymn or worship song that comes to mind.

Instead of Comparing, Try This!

:: ANGELA THOMAS ::

*But seek first his kingdom and his righteousness,
and all these things will be given to you as well.*

MATTHEW 6:33 NIV

*T*here I was in my gym shorts, hair in a ponytail, and no makeup at my son's after-school soccer game. I was just thankful to have made it on time after the crazy day I'd had. The kids had been to doctors' appointments. I'd been working on a writing deadline and I'd even been to the gym for a quick workout. Standing beside that soccer field, I was actually feeling pretty accomplished, until I did what I know not to do. I looked around.

The other moms looked fresh as daisies. They had re-membered to bring soccer chairs. I had forgotten. They had individually wrapped snacks for their other children. My kids were starving. And the unfair comparison began in my head.

You know how unfair comparison goes. You have no idea about someone else's story so you make one up for them and believe it. Then you stack your own story beside theirs and every single time you unfairly compare, you give the prize of living a great life to the other person. I've done it too many times. But I know better.

That day, it was as if the Lord spoke to me. "Have you been living My story for you today? Seeking Me first for your family and schedule and heart?" I honestly told Him I had tried to live for Him all day long. "Well then, ponytail girl, you have done all that I asked for today. Seeking Me is the only measure you need. Now go bless those other ladies with a sweet hello."

Every time I begin to compare myself to someone else's calling, the striving begins. But when I remember that God has called me to seek Him first, my obedience to Him brings peace.

> *Father, I pray for us all, may we seek You today in*
> *every encounter, every detail, and every decision.*
> *Let Your kingdom be our only purpose. Keep our*
> *hearts full of Your presence and Your peace. So very*
> *amen and amen.*

REFLECTION: Today, may you and I seek first the kingdom and turn away from the unfair comparison.

Journal, sketch, compose a poem, write a letter to God,
meditate on a hymn or worship song that comes to mind.

Life's Gardener

:: JANET DAVIS ::

Which of you fathers, if your son asks for a fish,
will give him a snake instead? Or if he asks
for an egg, will give him a scorpion?

LUKE 11:11–12 NIV

*I*n the spring of 2005, I found myself tending someone else's garden. Our twenty-three-year-old son, Bob, and I were spending eight weeks in a rented condominium on Beacon Hill in Boston. We were there so Bob could receive proton beam radiation at nearby Massachusetts General Hospital for a brain tumor that had been diagnosed during his first week of law school the previous fall.

Now "tending" is probably a generous description of what I was doing . . . removing a few dead leaves and branches. Better said, I was observing.

Each morning I noted what new spot of green had broken ground. As the sun became warmer and longer in the sky, hidden wonders were responding according to their own intrinsic rhythms.

I didn't know what the blooms would be. I recognized the shape of a hyacinth but could only guess its color. The same with what looked to be a tulip. I eagerly anticipated each revelation with excitement.

Brushing dirt away from a new shoot one day, I thought, "Tending someone else's garden is a lot like life: You never know what's going to come up next. Why is it that I don't respond in the same optimistic way to life's uncertain reality as I do to this one?" Perhaps my struggle is not simply uncertainty. Maybe there is a deeper issue here.

Perhaps it is a matter of trusting the goodness and intent of the gardener. I trusted that the owner had not planted poison ivy or thorns. Without fear, I anticipated only good. Though certainly there would be weeds, I was confident they would be manageable.

Things were different on the journey with the tumor. Did I trust that God would never give me more than I could endure? Harder still: Would I believe that for my children? Do I trust the goodness and intent of life's Gardener?

How different my life would look if (when?) I choose to live the uncertainty of life with the same delightful anticipation, wonder, and celebration I have found tending someone else's garden.

I believe, God, help my unbelief.

REFLECTION: How do you generally respond to uncertainty? Fear, delightful anticipation, ambivalence?

*Journal, sketch, compose a poem, write a letter to God,
meditate on a hymn or worship song that comes to mind.*

God Meets the Empty-Handed with His Mercy

:: ROSALIE DE ROSSET ::

Hear me, O Lord; for thy lovingkindness is good; turn unto me according to the multitude of thy tender mercies.

PSALM 69:16 KJV

We may sometimes be unaware of how God shows His mercy. A friend recently told me a story about God's small, tender mercies. Plagued by the threat of job loss and the management indifference that often goes with such situations, she also had a series of unexpected expenses: a garage roof weakened by interminable winter snow, the failure of major appliances, and car repair. Exhausted and frightened, she nevertheless determined to believe that God was in the details of her life. However, our faith waxes and wanes, and some days, she said, she could hardly face one more torturous hour of feeling insignificant, invisible . . . one more morning of wondering what lay ahead. Fear crouched at her door. And then God intervened.

54

For Christmas she had received a pair of beautiful cashmere gloves, gloves she loved for their color, warmth, and luxury. Arriving home one night, she noticed that one glove was simply gone, a loss we all know. Ugly things are seldom lost—only our favorite items. Deeply discouraged, she retraced her steps—to the gas station, the grocery store, the office. No glove. The days went on, dogged by the same complexities. Sometimes she looked ahead with hope—at other times she was just tired.

Leaving the office one evening, she saw only a few cars in the garage. Hers sat by itself. As she came to the right of her vehicle, she inadvertently (was it really an accident?) glanced at the ground only to see what looked like a piece of fabric. Then, to her amazement, she realized it was the cashmere glove, untorn and unsoiled—two full weeks after she had lost it. This, she understood immediately, was not coincidence but orchestrated by a God who shows up in the details, the God who whispers, "Take heart, My child." This was a small and very tender mercy.

The late poet Denise Levertov calls such mercies God's "untraced interventions . . . discovered at the door by someone at wit's end returning home empty-handed after a day of looking for work."

> *Oh God, keep us aware that You are merciful, and in light of that, keep us courageous.*

REFLECTION: Create a small journal for the express purpose of writing down the blessings of God.

Journal, sketch, compose a poem, write a letter to God, meditate on a hymn or worship song that comes to mind.

Courageous Dreaming

:: SUSIE LARSON ::

God can do anything, you know—far more
than you could ever imagine or guess or
request in your wildest dreams!

EPHESIANS 3:20 THE MESSAGE

udson Taylor once wrote: "I have found there are three stages to every great work of God: first it is impossible, then it is difficult, then it is done." God wants us to dream with Him.

And yet, every time I've stepped out to reach for my dreams, I've encountered many mixed emotions along the way. One minute I'm excited, the next minute I'm scared out of my mind. One minute I have faith, and the next, I am consumed by doubt.

If you have dared to venture with God to a new place, you've no doubt encountered a few contradicting emotions on your journey.

When the dream is far away, we experience intermingled feelings of excitement and impatience. But when the dream is finally within our grasp and it touches our *humanness*—we become especially aware of our own potential to make a mess of things—and that's unsettling to say the least.

The phases of our "dream-come-true" journey often look like this:

A Dream Far Off—Exciting, waiting, wondering, impatient.

A Dream Up Close—Fear, second-guessing ourselves, stepping out of our known zone into the learning zone. Wondering about the cost now that the dream is so close. Wondering if God made a mistake in choosing us. We can't go back—we're not the same after having this dream—but feeling unsure and unsteady about moving forward.

A Dream Realized—Once we take the land and we find a new normal, we become more seasoned and strengthened to stand in this place. But it's not without effort, faith, and occasional fatigue. We wouldn't have it any other way, and yet, no one but God knows what it took for us to step out like we did. *This* is the life of faith.

> *Lord, I want to dream big with You! Give me faith and help me to walk forward unafraid! I am willing to be stretched and strengthened for Your purposes. I want to experience the miracle of Your life at work within me. In Jesus' Name I pray, Amen.*

REFLECTION: Are you living a self-protective life? What God-sized dream is hidden within you?

Journal, sketch, compose a poem, write a letter to God, meditate on a hymn or worship song that comes to mind.

How Well Do I Know the Holy Spirit?

:: VINITA HAMPTON WRIGHT ::

> *No one comprehends what is truly God's except the*
> *Spirit of God. Now we have received not the spirit of*
> *the world, but the Spirit that is from God, so that we*
> *may understand the gifts bestowed on us by God.*

1 CORINTHIANS 2:11–12 NRSV

*M*ost of us who grew up in a Christian environment learn early that the Holy Spirit dwells within a person who has placed her faith in Jesus Christ. In some circles we talk about the Holy Spirit quite a lot. But it's surprising how easily we forget this holy presence that resides in our souls. In fact, we tend to live as if all the spiritual help we need lies *outside* us.

It's true that God is indeed Creator and therefore separate from us, the creation. But God is also *within* us through the presence of the Holy Spirit. What does this mean? It means that we are usually wiser than we realize. We possess the inner resource of wisdom given to us by God. The Holy Spirit is at work within our spirit, teaching us and then reminding us of what we know. God's wisdom becomes intricately connected to our thoughts and problem solving, our emotions and intuitions.

What this means is that when we pray for wisdom and discernment, it is appropriate for us to search within our own hearts and minds for the wisdom and discernment the Holy Spirit continually develops there. When we pay attention to our intuition, our logic, and our emotional responses, we are acknowledging that, *Yes, the Holy Spirit does dwell right here and is working within me.*

Do we truly believe that we are a new creation in Christ? That our hearts and minds are being renewed day by day? If so, then it's time to live in the truth of that renewal. It's time to trust that the Holy Spirit is doing what Jesus promised He would do—dwelling in us and guiding us.

> *Holy Spirit, thank You for dwelling in my soul as comforter, teacher, and spiritual companion. Open my spiritual eyes to Your constant presence in my life. Amen.*

REFLECTION: How will my prayer life change if, every time I pray, I acknowledge the Holy Spirit's active presence in my thoughts, hopes, emotions, and memories?

Journal, sketch, compose a poem, write a letter to God, meditate on a hymn or worship song that comes to mind.

What Are People Telling Me, about Me?

:: LORI NEFF ::

Instead, we will speak the truth in love,
growing in every way more and more like Christ,
who is the head of his body, the church.

EPHESIANS 4:15 NLT

I recently received the coolest gift ever. Anita made creative cards for Melinda and me—a different card per week for a year. Some cards have words and pictures, and others have questions. She put these cards together in a beautiful box and made us promise to not look ahead! This week's card has different words that came to mind when Anita thinks of me. What an encouragement to see that she had written things such as "creative," "organized," and "intelligent"! It reminded me of the importance of hearing specific, encouraging truth from people close to us.

Sometimes there are characteristics that come so naturally we can't see them for ourselves and we need someone close to reflect back to us what they see. Are you like me? I often think, *Wow, that person just did something great.* But I don't often translate that into a kind, truthful spoken word. Does your friend show courage in a difficult relationship? Tell her! Did your husband show compassion in a beautiful way? Let him know that you loved seeing that quality displayed! Is your quiet coworker one of the hardest working, consistent people you know? How about sending a note to say that you notice?

Hearing what others see can be more than encouraging (though that is valuable); it can also help us become more self-aware and know how God has gifted us. We might think of "speaking the truth in love" as a verse that relates only to speaking the difficult things—but, what about speaking up about the good things? That's truth that needs to be spoken too. Not with flattery, but truth spoken with love. Why not encourage one person each day this week (and even make it a lifelong practice)?

> *Loving Father, please help me to speak the truth in love this week.*

REFLECTION: What is something that other people tell you about yourself? Is God calling you to act on that truth in a deeper way?

Journal, sketch, compose a poem, write a letter to God, meditate on a hymn or worship song that comes to mind.

Why Is Confession So Hard?

:: GINGER KOLBABA ::

Cleanse me with hyssop, and I will be clean;
wash me, and I will be whiter than snow.

PSALM 51:7 NIV

C onfession.

Why is it so difficult for us when it's so good for us?

For me, sometimes I don't want to confess something, because I know if I confess, then I have to change. And sometimes, I don't want to change. I want to hold on to that negative attitude or unforgiving spirit or sinful behavior. Not always, but there are moments when the transformation God calls me to is way beyond where I'm ready or willing to go.

But God can't work in my life or the lives of others or the church or our world when I cling tightly to those things that keep the distance between God and me. So I confess. I admit how far I am from God's perfect and holy standard.

And in those daily—sometimes hourly!—moments of admission, I find that God shows up, arms flung open just like the father whose Prodigal Son returned, and He embraces me and fills me with peace and joy and His glory.

And I change.

In confession, we change. And the church changes. And the world transforms. All because we—Christians who are forgiven—step out in faith and confess our desperate need for a Savior.

As Christ-followers, we're the role models for showing others what confession looks like. Because showing our brokenness makes our restoration and wholeness that much more precious and wonderful and enticing.

Will you join me and confess? Will you be exposed for the world to see the true power of forgiveness and freedom? Oh, what amazing things God can do through us, the church, when we do! Imagine the joy of being whiter than snow.

> *Father, forgive me for the times I've clung tightly to the things that I should confess. Help me to focus on the feelings of freedom and joy that accompany redemption rather than on the fear and anxiety that hold me captive when I don't come clean.*

REFLECTION: What are some things that you struggle with confessing? How do you ultimately feel once you let them go and acknowledge them to God?

Journal, sketch, compose a poem, write a letter to God, meditate on a hymn or worship song that comes to mind.

Her Unplanned Pregnancy

:: ANGIE WESZELY ::

*Speak and act as those who are going to be
judged by the law that gives freedom,
because judgment without mercy will be
shown to anyone who has not been merciful.*

JAMES 2:12–13 NIV

When I found out this was a Christian organization, I was like, oh great. Here we go. I didn't want to hear about religion. That makes you feel even worse."

This nineteen-year-old woman was convinced Christians would only cause her more pain as she wrestled with the decision of whether or not to end her pregnancy. She is not alone in her feelings. Many women facing unplanned pregnancy don't bother coming to Christians for help, but instead go straight to an abortion clinic. If a woman doesn't trust us to help her, we have no way to help the child. But it doesn't have to be this way. We can see mercy triumph over judgment in this issue, and it begins with focusing on the needs of the woman.

A woman facing an unplanned pregnancy often experiences overwhelming feelings of shame, panic, and isolation that threaten her very identity. By the time that little line turns pink, she is crushed under the sense that her life as she knows it is now over, and everything inside her cries out for a way to change this desperate situation. In order for her to trust others enough to ask for help, she needs comfort, acceptance, and someone to listen to her without judgment.

And we can do this. We can listen to a woman, try to understand what is going on when she is considering abortion, and empathize with why she would feel overwhelmed to be nineteen—or whatever age—and pregnant. We can consider the judgment she is already receiving from others and refuse to treat her mistake as worse than any sin of our own. We can extend to her the same mercy God extends to us.

God, remind me of how You show mercy to me every day, and help me to be merciful toward women who are facing unplanned pregnancy. Use me to reflect Your compassionate heart for both the woman and the child.

REFLECTION: Ask youself, Would a woman facing an unplanned pregnancy find me safe to approach? Do I listen, understand, empathize, extend mercy? Write a prayer asking God to help you be that person.

Journal, sketch, compose a poem, write a letter to God, meditate on a hymn or worship song that comes to mind.

Sand Dollar Prayers

:: TRISH BERG ::

*"What do you want me to do for you?" Jesus asked
him. The blind man said, "Rabbi, I want to see."*

MARK 10:51 NIV

*L*ast summer, my husband, Michael, and I packed our
cooler full of food, our minivan full of luggage, and
our hearts full of hope as we mapped out a road trip
from our Ohio farmhouse to Bar Harbor, Maine, with our four
children.

We ate seafood, hiked in Acadia National Park, and
watched the sunset from the pier. But my most extraordinary
memory came from a surprising answered prayer.

On the way home, we picnicked at Old Orchard Beach.
Our children collected seashells and searched hard for sand
dollars. After a couple of hours, they screamed with delight
when they finally found one. As the sun set, they were determined to find more.

We decided to take one last walk along the shore to the
pier. I began to pray for more sand dollars because I knew my

daughters each wanted one to keep. I prayed and I walked and I looked.

Then I heard Sydney screech with joy. She found one! We all hugged like schoolgirls—until I noticed my younger daughter, Riley, looking forlorn since she was the only girl without a sand dollar. I prayed for yet another sand dollar.

I took a single step, and there it was, right near my foot. I felt as if God had smiled down on us that day and His presence was unmistakable.

I felt like Bartimaeus, the blind beggar, who shouted boldly for Jesus to answer his prayer. Just as Bartimaeus did not shy away, I did not shy away from my simple, sand dollar prayer.

Most days, I pray halfheartedly. I hide my simple requests underneath insecurity and timidity. But God wants us to pray like Bartimaeus, to be bold in our faith.

So pack your life full of love, your faith full of expectations, and your heart full of hope as you map out each day. God wants you to bring your mundane, sand dollar prayers to the foot of the cross and then trust in Him for the answer.

> *Dear Lord, help me to boldly walk by faith and*
> *grace, trusting You to answer my sand dollar*
> *prayers.*

REFLECTION: What sand dollar prayers are you hiding from God?

Journal, sketch, compose a poem, write a letter to God,
meditate on a hymn or worship song that comes to mind.

The God Who Sees

:: SANDRA GLAHN ::

She gave this name to the Lord who spoke to her:
"You are the God who sees me," for she said,
"I have now seen the One who sees me."

GENESIS 16:13 NIV

O f all the studies on Bible women I've completed, only
one included Hagar. And it viewed her as Sarah's failure
in the baby department.

Hagar belongs on the "she-roes" list. As Sarah's Egyptian
slave, Hagar started out with both race and class against her.
Yet once she conceived Abraham's child, her status changed.
That led to a power shift, and she despised Sarah. (If someone made me bear a child and took it, I'd resent her, too.)

Sarah mistreated Hagar so badly that she fled to the
desert (Genesis 16), where the Lord's angel found her by a
well. And though He sent Hagar back, He also made some
amazing promises.

He promised to multiply Hagar's offspring. She's the only
woman in Scripture to receive such a promise. He told her to

name her baby "God listens." He promised that Ishmael would be "a wild donkey of a man." Though "donkey" is an insult in our world, remember what Jesus rode during His triumphal entry. And to be "wild" wasn't to be crazy but "free." Our equivalent: "You'll return to slavery, but your offspring will be free stallions."

God promised that Hagar's son would dwell in the presence of his brothers. By their proximity to Israel, Arabs witness up close God's unfolding plan. The same texts promising restoration to a Jewish remnant (Isaiah 60:1–5) predict the restoration of a greater remnant among Abraham's Arabian descendants (vv. 6–7).

What was Hagar's response to all this? She gave the Lord a name: *El Roi*—the God who sees.

From her we learn that God is sovereign over wombs and nations; that He has a plan for both Jew and Arab; that He is a husband to the husbandless; that He hears the cries of the mistreated; and that He is the God who sees.

> *Thank You, Lord, that You are a good God, that You sent Your Son for us, that You defend the defenseless, that You see everything, even me and all my needs.*

REFLECTION: It's easy to feel invisible and alone. Right now where do you need to be reminded that God sees you?

Journal, sketch, compose a poem, write a letter to God, meditate on a hymn or worship song that comes to mind.

Becoming God's Empowered Woman

:: LESLIE VERNICK ::

On the seventh day of the feast, when King Xerxes was in high spirits because of the wine, he told the seven eunuchs who attended him . . . to bring Queen Vashti to him with the royal crown on her head. He wanted the nobles and all the other men to gaze on her beauty, for she was a very beautiful woman. But when they conveyed the king's order to Queen Vashti, she refused to come.

ESTHER 1:10–12 NLT

hy did it take me fifty years to wire up enough courage to stand up for myself?" Sara asked, sighing. "I've always put everyone else first. Now I understand that I've only enabled my husband's selfishness to flourish."

From a young age, many women are trained to give, to go along and to not hurt anyone's feelings at all costs. "Be nice," we're told, "or people won't like you." We've learned to please, to placate, and to pretend in order to not make waves, just to keep the peace.

Before marriage and after, I was told to obey authority and to submit to my husband, even if his requests seemed foolish or harmful. Passivity seemed to be the biblical definition of a gentle and quiet (feminine) spirit.

Yet the Scriptures reveal many women who were strong and stood firm. They didn't always obey or submit. They sometimes said no. Queen Vashti is one of my favorites. She refused to allow herself to be treated as a sexual object for her husband's friends to ogle. Another woman, Queen Esther, approached the same king hoping to right a terrible wrong though she knew she could face expulsion or execution for her boldness.

Scriptures tell the story of Abigail, a wife who overruled her husband's foolishness and took charge when her family faced the wrath of David and his men (1 Samuel 25). Earlier in Jewish history we find two midwives who refused to obey the pharaoh's orders to murder Hebrew babies (Exodus 1:17).

In a culture where females were often devalued and disrespected, God empowered women to stand up for themselves, for others, and for what was right.

Lord, give us the courage to stand up and say no
when it is necessary.

REFLECTION: Identify the times that you have been too nice, too accommodating, or too passive. What has it cost you?

Journal, sketch, compose a poem, write a letter to God,
meditate on a hymn or worship song that comes to mind.

Growing "Old" or Growing "New"?

:: JAN SILVIOUS ::

*Therefore we do not lose heart. Though
outwardly we are wasting away, yet inwardly
we are being renewed day by day.*

2 CORINTHIANS 4:16 NIV

I was in a shop in a sleepy Southern town. As I browsed through the good smelling potpourri, the wonderful candles and ornaments, and the clever signs (that always seem to mean more in the shop than on your desk at home), I noticed this statement: "Act old later." It yelled at me: "Save it! Don't go there. There will be time enough later on. If you aren't on your last leg today, don't act like it."

It is true that we can talk ourselves into feeling bad and acting old. This can happen no matter what age we are. I've seen twenty-year-olds "act old" with a cold. I've seen middle-aged women act as if menopause is going to kill them, and I've seen seasoned women turn into little old ladies just by telling themselves they are rickety, aged specimens of humanity.

I've seen in my own life that my conversation with myself can set the tone of a whole day. If I believe that it's going to be miserable, it usually is miserable but if I can see it as an adventure, it will be an adventure! Even when we have to do something we just don't like, if we can tell ourselves "I may not like this but God knows I'm here and I'm being made new," it can change the whole tenor of the day.

The truth is that no matter how old we are or what's going on, we are being "renewed" every day. We don't have to embrace the "old, run-down" message. If we are being made new, then there is something fresh and wonderful about each day, no matter how old we are. It is our job to embrace it and believe it.

> *Lord, keep me from buying into the message that I*
> *am "old and run-down." Keep me reminded that You*
> *are making me new and fresh each day. May my*
> *eyes be opened to what You have for me this day.*
> *Amen.*

REFLECTION: Recognize that God is doing something "new" in your life today? What words that age you will you take out of your vocabulary?

Journal, sketch, compose a poem, write a letter to God,
meditate on a hymn or worship song that comes to mind.

My Self-Loathing Needs to Stop!

:: KARYN PURVIS ::

Glorify the Lord with me . . .
PSALM 34:3 NIV

When I was a young child in south Texas, one of my most intriguing Christmas gifts was a microscope. Colorful wrappings were barely torn from the present before I dashed to our backyard in search of treasures to view under the powerful scope. With great delight I found a butterfly wing and raced to put it under the magnification. As I eagerly put my eye to the viewer and gained a first glance at my treasure, I was captivated at the appearance of the wing that looked so astonishingly different under the powerful magnification. That crisp Christmas morning, I spent hours finding new treasures and looking at them under my microscope, but that first stunning image of a butterfly wing had become deeply etched in my memory.

Years later, as a young woman, on one particularly gloomy night, I found myself filled with self-loathing for my weaknesses and failures. I found myself ruminating on silly things I had said, on embarrassing things I had done, on my human frailties, and on each disappointing imperfection of my life.

In the midst of my dark pondering, I began to reflect on the focus of my thinking—it was all about me! In God's mercies, a verse came to me: "Oh magnify the Lord with me!"— and with the verse came an image of my childhood microscope and the amazing beauty and clarity of that butterfly wing. By an act of my will, I shifted attention to the glorious detail of God's face, seeing Him and His great love in full magnification. In an instant my dark thoughts yielded to His glory! The metaphor of that night has carried me many times and I am reminded to magnify Him!

> *Holy, sovereign God, today, help me look deeply*
> *into Your eyes and see Your great love and Your*
> *great mercies toward me. Empower me, Lord, to*
> *turn my eyes fully toward You and to find joy and*
> *peace in Your presence.*

REFLECTION: In what ways do I look at myself and others, seeing through critical eyes that magnify failures and weaknesses? As I look into God's eyes and see His goodness and His love, in what practical ways can I see myself and those around me through His eyes?

Journal, sketch, compose a poem, write a letter to God,
meditate on a hymn or worship song that comes to mind.

Tending the Soul

SECTION TWO

Getting to Know Ourselves through Creative Self-Expression

:: MELINDA SCHMIDT ::

First this: God created the Heavens and Earth—
all you see, all you don't see.

GENESIS 1:1 THE MESSAGE

*C*reativity. What reaction did you just have when you read that one word?

"Oooooh no. If she's going to talk about creativity, I'm outta here! Let's see what's on the next page."

Or,

"Oooooh, this sounds fun—now, where is my acid-free glue stick?"

In her book *Resting Place*, Jane Rubietta writes, "None of us stood behind the door when God doled out creativity." And why would we think we could escape being gifted by God with our portion of creativity?

Creativity doesn't only come in an acid-free glue stick, paintbrush, or jar of Mod Podge. We know creativity is in a garden plot, a closet or finances organized, a gizmo repaired, a Girl Scout badge completed, computer files managed, helping our kids build scenery for the school play, an orderly basement (not my gift!), cream puffs stuffed with chocolate, or a charitable event planned for Haiti earthquake relief.

Is your God-gifted creativity quietly resting, waiting to be engaged? Might your creativity apathy be keeping you from engaging with your own Creator in new ways?

> *God, I want to know You as Creator and know my*
> *own creativity in new ways. Help me to have the*
> *courage, take the time, and make the effort to see*
> *Your creativity in the day before me and around me,*
> *and to know I have something creative to add!*

REFLECTION: Journaling is also creativity and can restart the creative process. "The word God has been whispering to me lately is . . ." "My fears and disappointments right now are . . ." "God, these days I am fumbling with . . ." Begin to think about, *What is blocking my creativity? How can I take a next courageous step?*

Journal, sketch, compose a poem, write a letter to God,
meditate on a hymn or worship song that comes to mind.

Impressions

:: ELLIE KAY ::

*If you spend yourselves in behalf of the hungry and
satisfy the needs of the oppressed, then your light
will rise in the darkness, and your night
will become like the noonday.*

ISAIAH 58:10 NIV

*O*ne Saturday afternoon, a woman named Cindy was driving down Main Street in her town. In her trunk, she had four bags of groceries. While stopped at a crosswalk, she noticed that the woman crossing the street was blind and assisted by four young children. They pushed a metal cart with one small bag of groceries, and Cindy assumed they just came from the nearby supermarket.

Suddenly, a still, small voice spoke to her heart and said, *Stop your car and give them your groceries.* Cindy had never had thoughts like this before and didn't know how to respond.

Again, the impression was clear. *Give them all of your groceries. It's your blessing to keep or refuse.*

So she turned her car around, found the young family,

and ran to them with the groceries in her arms. As she placed the bags in their metal cart, she said, "I know you don't know me and that's not important. What is important is that you know that God loves you and He wants you to have these groceries."

The woman was overwhelmed at the thought of a God who loved her so much that He would send a stranger to meet her need. She began to cry. The children began to rifle through the bags of groceries. "Look, Mama, there's milk, we can have milk with our cereal! There's also juice and fruit!" Then the youngest said something a mother of a toddler never wants to hear, "And dere's eben GUM!"

The woman sobbed. "Thank you! Oh, *bless you!*"

While Cindy was in the store earlier that day, buying groceries for her family, God had another woman in mind. As she purchased milk and gum, He was using her to be a blessing to others.

Lord, open my eyes to the needs of others. Amen.

REFLECTION: This week watch for someone whose need God can use you to meet.

Journal, sketch, compose a poem, write a letter to God, meditate on a hymn or worship song that comes to mind.

Dependence

:: BARB LARIMORE ::

For in him we live and move and have our being.
ACTS 17:28 NIV

Anna. Blonde, wispy hair. Bright blue eyes. Thirty-six inches tall; twenty-eight pounds; thirty months old. Daughter. Big sister. My first grand-child and the apple of her daddy's eye. Sugar and spice and everything nice. I love holding her, reading to her, hugging her, walking with her, caring for her, feeding her, praying with her, and putting her to bed. And, this week, I *loved* being on vacation with her—as God used her to teach *me* a powerful lesson.

It occurred after I heard little Anna say, time after time, things such as: "Daddy carry me," "Daddy do it," "Daddy fix it," "Where's Daddy?" Followed by, "I want my daddy!" The latter would occur whenever she had a stumble accompanied by an abrasion or a bump or a bruise.

This was the epiphany I had through Anna: Isn't this the way God wants *us* to live?

Anna lives in total dependence on her stay-at-home daddy. He gladly meets her every need. He is her provider and protector. He knows the nuances of her voice and she knows his.

Her father, her *abba*, skillfully guides her through her daily schedule, from early morning until bedtime, giving her food, drink, rest, and playtime.

Her daddy would go to the ends of the earth for this little girl.

And so would our heavenly Father, our Abba, and our heavenly Daddy—for you and for me.

> *Father, help me to live, move, and have my very*
> *being in total dependence upon You daily.*

REFLECTION: Thinking about your own father may be difficult. Spend some time journaling about the attributes of God and the truth of those character traits even if they are not true of your earthly father. Imagine your life if you'd had the father you needed. How does God relate to you in those ways?

Journal, sketch, compose a poem, write a letter to God,
meditate on a hymn or worship song that comes to mind.

Thankful in Every Circumstance

:: SIBYL TOWNER ::

Be joyful always; pray continually;
give thanks in all circumstances, for this is
God's will for you in Christ Jesus.

1 THESSALONIANS 5:16–18 NIV

Mother's Day 1966. My mother had died several weeks before at the age of fifty-one. This began events that would change the direction of my life as a mother of two young sons.

Three months later my stepfather died suddenly, leaving my four younger brothers and sisters without parents and without a place to go, as no provision had been made for them. They were thirteen, fifteen, sixteen, and eighteen. We were led by God to include them into our family and became their legal guardian. This meant letting go of the way we were living and of the way we thought that our lives would unfold.

What we had no way of knowing was that the house that we found allowed my gifts of hospitality to flourish. The property provided space for my husband to garden. We knew that the home we were in was entrusted to us by God and that it was not our own and that we were to steward it and make it available as He asked us. We lived in that home for twenty-seven years, and as my siblings grew up and left, God brought other young adults to our doorstep. We hosted sixty-seven young people in that home, some for three months and some for several years. Even my grandmother, at age eighty-nine, came to our home to visit and then said she liked our home and would like to stay . . . and stay she did till she went home to the Lord when she was ninety-five.

The above Scripture became our life verse early in our marriage, and while we were not thankful *for* every circumstance, we began the practice of being thankful *in* every circumstance. After forty-eight years of living this text, it has become the foundation of our home and is embedded in the DNA of who we are and who we are continuing to become. It is our witness to Christ alive and at work in the day-to-day circumstances of our lives.

> *Dear Father, help me to know that in all things You will work for good. Help me to trust that today.*

REFLECTION: Get outside, take a walk, and reflect on God's goodness through the years.

Journal, sketch, compose a poem, write a letter to God, meditate on a hymn or worship song that comes to mind.

"Whoohoo!"

:: ROBIN CHADDOCK ::

Call to me and I will answer you.
I'll tell you marvelous and wondrous things
that you could never figure out on your own.

JEREMIAH 33:3 THE MESSAGE

A friend of mine gave a talk this past year that made a huge difference in my life. She talked about a morning ritual, a prayer of sorts, that she and her five-year-old son engage in.

She gets up first and spends some time in quiet. The end of that quiet is signaled by her son waking up and standing at the top of the stairs. She knows he's there because he calls, "Whoohoo . . ."

She answers "Whoohoo . . ." And then they snuggle for a few minutes.

She likened this to a lovely way to encounter God in prayer, and I really resonated!

Sometimes we forget that God is our Abba Father, who said, "I'm no longer calling you servants . . . No, I've named you friends" (John 15:15 THE MESSAGE). Because Jesus is Immanuel—God with us—we can enjoy that respectful and deeply loving relationship with Him that He desires to have with His beloved creatures.

I have been drawn to this practice, this perspective in prayer, of quietly spending time with God, of being in His company, especially when I'm feeling vulnerable, a bit lost, or just need to have some deep soul rest. I'm so prone to big, go-go-go life that sometimes I just need some pure and simple tender loving care. This approach to prayer has actually become the "marvelous and wondrous thing that you could never figure out on your own."

I haven't often understood the truly loving, friendly, caring nature of God. I haven't embraced God as God embraces me. But thinking of my friend's "Whoohoos" has really shifted my notions about my Creator. It's kinda cool.

> *Hello God, Sometimes I just need Your gentle friendship and Your loving hug. Sometimes I need just a simple solution or a unspectacular bit of guidance. The marvelous and wondrous, when I come right down to it, is indeed Your tender care, Your fabulous friendship, the warmth of Your smile, and Your touch. Thank You for this deeper level of genuine communion with You. In anticipation, Amen.*

REFLECTION: What is your image of, your belief about, the God to whom you are praying?

Journal, sketch, compose a poem, write a letter to God, meditate on a hymn or worship song that comes to mind.

What Does God See in Me?

:: JENA MORROW ::

*For we are God's masterpiece. He has created us
anew in Christ Jesus, so we can do the good things
he planned for us long ago.*

EPHESIANS 2:10 NLT

hen you look at yourself in the mirror in the morning, what do you see? Do you see flaws, imperfections, "problem areas"? Do you see evidence of time having marched on, of stress having had its merciless way with you? Do you see laugh lines or frown lines? Which would you *rather* see?

More importantly, when you look in the mirror, what do you say to yourself? Do you scold yourself for having "let yourself go"? Do you shame yourself for an extra inch or two here or there, for hair that isn't straight enough or curly enough or the right color or length? If you talk back to your reflection (and most of us do, silently), are the things you say to yourself things you might say to your girlfriend or your sister? Or are they so horrible and degrading that you reserve them only for yourself?

When God looks at you, He sees an image radically different from that which you see. You are God's masterpiece. Think about that for a minute—you, a work of art. A one-of-a-kind, bona fide original, hand-signed by the Artist. He chose your hair color, your skin tone, the shape of your eyes, the distinct character of your smile. None of it was an accident. None of it was unplanned. He never once said, "Oops."

The day we are able to look at our reflection in the mirror and appreciate it, even just for a moment, for what it is—an image of God's handiwork, imprinted with His love and approval—is the day we begin to heal.

> *Father God, help me to remember what Your holy, infallible Word says about me. Thank You for taking such care in creating my body; please help me to learn to care for my body, myself, as Your masterpiece .*

REFLECTION: Think about the word "masterpiece" for a moment. What comes to mind? If you were given a masterpiece for a gift, how would you treat it?

Journal, sketch, compose a poem, write a letter to God, meditate on a hymn or worship song that comes to mind.

Living in Illusion

:: ANDREA FABRY ::

Foolish dreamers live in a world of illusion;
wise realists plant their feet on the ground.

PROVERBS 14:18 THE MESSAGE

*T*had no idea we were living an illusion when we moved to Colorado in 2000. We were blissfully raising our large family. We had the typical marriage and family struggles, but nothing outside the norm.

We noticed health issues a few months after the move. Our nine children developed seizures, hearing loss, vision disturbance, auto immune disease, rashes, and digestive problems. Even our pets became ill. Despite a discovery of black mold in the house in 2007, we made no connection between our problems and our environment. Our health issues escalated. By October 2008 we had connected the dots and vacated our home.

"Treat the home as if it were on fire," we were advised. We left everything. Our possessions, pets, and cherished memories. But the real test was relinquishing our illusions.

Those were buried deep beneath my false assumptions. We would raise happy, healthy children, pay off our mortgage, and live Christ-honoring lives.

That was an illusion.

We now live in the desert in our fifth rental home. I struggle daily with the drudgery and demands of the recovery process. Our future has never been so uncertain.

But there's something better than immunity from life's pain. A paid-off house and a clean bill of health will never buy eternity.

Jesus taught us to see what is real in life. Not the illusion. He taught us to focus on the unseen, on what is eternal. When we base our life on reality, our foundation doesn't drift or evaporate or crumble.

If you're having a hard time with the way things "are" in your life, it may be that God is stripping the illusions away, taking those things you might be tempted to trust in instead of Him. Don't fight the process. Look for the hidden reality beneath your circumstances. You'll find yourself firmly planted on solid ground.

Father, it's so easy to live by illusion. Show us our subtle lies. Help us walk confidently in the knowledge that You alone provide our security. You alone can provide solid footing in a shaky world.

REFLECTION: Is there any illusion that you're holding on to today?

Journal, sketch, compose a poem, write a letter to God, meditate on a hymn or worship song that comes to mind.

Expressions of Our Faith

:: HELEN LEE ::

Is not this the kind of fasting I have chosen: to loose
the chains of injustice and untie the cords of the yoke,
to set the oppressed free and break every yoke?
Is it not to share your food with the hungry and to
provide the poor wanderer with shelter—
when you see the naked, to clothe him, and not to turn
away from your own flesh and blood? . . . Then you
will call, and the Lord will answer; you will
cry for help, and he will say: Here am I.

ISAIAH 58:6–7, 9 NIV

I generally try to live a good Christian life. I read the Bible and pray, I go to church, I tithe, I try to teach my kids about Jesus, I serve when and where I can. But then I read these words from Isaiah. I felt that God was clearly speaking to me, challenging me to redefine my ideas about what the "good Christian life" was all about, just as He questioned the Israelites about whether their efforts at fasting were in fact what He wanted from them.

Fasting and other Christian disciplines such as prayer, meditation, and attending church are all important activities for Christians to pursue and can certainly strengthen our relationship with God. But if we are feeling disconnected from God, if our relationship with Him seems stilted somehow, perhaps these words from Isaiah can help us find the answer. God admonishes the Israelites to pursue different expressions of their faith than fasting—such as seeking after justice, feeding the hungry, and clothing the poor. And as they begin to bring God's love to others in these ways, the Lord says, "Here am I." We experience a much deeper sense of His presence as we live out His mission to be His hands and feet in a world that so desperately needs it.

God, forgive us if we have been too busy engaging in Christian activities to see Your heart for those who are suffering and struggling. Help us to embrace Your call to serve and love others, especially those who are poor, naked, or hungry.

REFLECTION: Make a list of ways to show love to those who are suffering and in need. What are the needs in your community that God could use you to meet?

Journal, sketch, compose a poem, write a letter to God, meditate on a hymn or worship song that comes to mind.

Gentle Whisper

:: LORRAINE PINTUS ::

Through Jesus, therefore, let us continually
offer to God a sacrifice of praise—
the fruit of lips that confess his name.

HEBREWS 13:15 NIV

*I*f I'm honest, this is one of those verses I'd like to rip out of my Bible. Most days praising God comes easily; my gratitude list is long. But some days it's hard— days when there's more on my schedule than is humanly possible to accomplish, and the car breaks down, and my kids have a meltdown, and I go to an important meeting unaware that I'm wearing one black shoe and one brown shoe (hey, if the shoe fits, I buy it in every color!). Add a toxic mix of wacked-out hormones to this day and I don't want to praise God—I want to smack something!

That's when God's gentle whisper reminds me: "Praise Me continually, Lorraine. Thank Me even when it's the last thing you feel like doing." "How God?" I ask. "How can I praise You when everything inside me wants to scream?" "Look again and you'll see the answer."

I read the verse and force my eyes to acknowledge the word I'd overlooked: sacrifice. To praise God when I don't feel like it is a sacrifice. I sacrifice my anger. I sacrifice my self-centeredness. I sacrifice my right to be right. I sacrifice my will; I take that stubborn rebel by the scruff of the neck and force it up on God's altar. "God, I offer myself to You. Pierce my will and let it die," I cry.

At times, a dead will is exactly what's needed. Once my will is out of the way, the Holy Spirit who indwells me is free to work. As the Spirit rises up and fills me, something amazing happens. My lips quiver. The words come out haltingly at first then with growing confidence: "I praise You, God. Even in this, I praise You."

> *Lord, I lay my will on Your altar. May I die to self and may You ignite my heart with Your Holy Spirit so that I might continually offer You what You deserve: A heart overflowing with praise.*

REFLECTION: Pull out some paper and crayons and have a conversation with God. See how you can praise Him through praying in color.

Journal, sketch, compose a poem, write a letter to God, meditate on a hymn or worship song that comes to mind.

God's Road Map

:: JENNIFER MARSHALL ::

When I think on my ways,
I turn my feet to your testimonies.

PSALM 119:59 ESV

Autopilot seems to move us along the first two decades of life. Third grade propels us into fourth, fourth into fifth, and so on. It's fairly easy to coast on autopilot all the way through college . . . and beyond.

So when reality takes a detour from the map of life we've got in mind, it can be quite a jolt.

In autopilot mode, we tend to focus on the next milestone—whether that's graduation, getting a job, getting married, having a baby, getting the kids through school, or retiring. When things don't come along on our time line, the discrepancy between expectations and actual experience can be disorienting.

What's more, focusing too much on the next milestone can cause us to dismiss or even despise the time between

milestones. But the in-between time is not throwaway time. Real life doesn't begin at the next milestone. It is here and now, and God has us exactly where He wants us for exactly as long as He wants us here.

God's road maps don't work like MapQuest where we get to choose our preferred route. God's route will likely take all kinds of inefficient turns and may leave us asking, "Why?" and "Are we there yet?" like children in the backseat during family road trips.

The challenge is to make wise plans while keeping a heart poised between what is, what we hope for, and what God actually will bring about for the future. Even as we long for the fulfillment of the desires of our hearts—whether marriage or children or a dream job—the here and now is significant.

Living with joy today while hopes remain unfulfilled depends on the conviction that there is a grand design to our lives.

That design is determined by our first call, to glorify and enjoy God—the single overriding purpose and pilot of our lives.

Father, give us a poise of heart to find joy and contentment today even as we have hopes that remain unfulfilled.

REFLECTION: How can we learn to embrace God's adventure for us even when it doesn't follow the map we've drawn up?

Journal, sketch, compose a poem, write a letter to God, meditate on a hymn or worship song that comes to mind.

Longing for Home

:: ANITA LUSTREA ::

*If they had longed for the country they came from,
they could have gone back. But they were looking for
a better place, a heavenly homeland. That is why
God is not ashamed to be called their God,
for he has prepared a city for them.*

HEBREWS 11:15–16 NLT

There I was sitting in Jimmy John's sandwich shop, tears streaming down my face, rock music blaring in the background, as I rummaged in my purse for a tissue. Home, that was the culprit! Nothing bad was happening at home. I hadn't had an argument with my husband. I wasn't even crying about a specific place or building called home. It was more a sense that I didn't belong. I've lived in eleven different houses, dorm rooms, and apartments in my lifetime, but none of those locales had brought me to tears. I was crying for the home I hadn't yet seen.

I've always envied people who were born, grew up, and died in the same town. There is something about a sense of place, a knowing and being known by a community of people

over the long haul that creates belonging. Isn't that what we all want, a place to belong?

In Hebrews chapter 11, the writer recounts a list of names that has come to be known as the Hall of Faith. These are names we know well from Scripture. Abraham, Sarah . . .

They all had something in common. They never felt fully at home where they lived, never felt like they fit in or fully belonged. Restlessness was part of the fabric of who they were. Ever felt that way? I did in Jimmy John's that day. I dried my tears and pulled my Bible out of the bag of books I had brought with me and turned to Hebrews 11 for a reminder that I wasn't alone in my longing for home. There were others who'd gone before me "looking for a better place, a heavenly homeland."

> *Oh God, when I feel alone, like I don't belong,*
> *please wrap Your arms around me and remind me*
> *that I don't belong in this world . . . but You have*
> *prepared a city for me, a heavenly homeland.*
> *Amen!*

REFLECTION: Write about or sketch what your heavenly homeland might look like. What will you do there?

Journal, sketch, compose a poem, write a letter to God,
meditate on a hymn or worship song that comes to mind.

Keep Banging the Drum

:: DONNA VANLIERE ::

*One day Jesus told his disciples a story to show
that they should always pray and never give up.*

LUKE 18:1 NLT

My friend Wendy was in a university marching band (if you're yawning, just wait!), and she told me some fascinating things.

She said that despite freezing or sweltering temperatures, band members maintained formation and kept playing. If a horse in front decided to take a potty break no one dodged the pile but stepped right in it. The band played on despite the noise from the crowd, the gnats in the air, or the mess in the road.

Welcome to life, huh? It seems most of us are pretty good at sustaining that rhythm of prayer when there's an emergency, but do we keep the beat going in the daily grind? If we did, would our lives exhibit more power, grace, or freedom through our continued cadence of worship? Jesus said to always pray and never give up, so it must be that our lives would be different! If we fully realized the power of that cadence, we'd keep marching even though we're hot and sticky. We'd sustain the rhythm right through the noise and distractions and despite the fact that we need to sit down for a while. I want that kind of prayer life—the kind where I don't throw in the towel but keep the beat of prayer going so I can dismantle the enemy's stronghold.

I know some of you are growing weary, but I encourage you to maintain cadence! Take your place in line with the other band members (some of them are within reach wearing their glittering, bedazzled uniforms). Look to your sisters around you and sustain the rhythm and unity of purpose even when it means you have to walk through a mess in front of you. Keep banging that drum and don't ever give up. Don't ever, ever, ever break cadence!

> *Lord, would You teach me how to pray? I never want to give up. Amen.*

REFLECTION: Ask a close friend to join you on a 30-day prayer experiment. Share requests and see what God will do.

Journal, sketch, compose a poem, write a letter to God, meditate on a hymn or worship song that comes to mind.

The Canvas

:: CINDY WEST ::

*Because of the Lord's great love we are
not consumed, for his compassions
never fail. They are new every morning . . .*

LAMENTATIONS 3:22–24 NIV

The artist's blank canvas. Place me in any local art store, and a grin appears on my face as my eyes scan the various sizes and shapes. Each one, its stretched, stark-white self, beckons to the artist, calling for the touch of a brush to bring forth color, texture, *life*.

I've discovered along my life's journey that my loving Father hands me a blank canvas each morning, one with the same invitation attached to it as those found in the art store. He knows the capacity of that canvas, the vibrancy of color that will appear from the moment I open my eyes until they close late at night. He has plans for me this day. Gifts for me to open. Good works for me to accomplish. Lessons for me to learn. On those days when I wield my paintbrush and engage—really engage by meticulously crafting each stroke—a masterpiece emerges. The day is declared complete.

I have the potential to live from a place of selfish pride instead of purposeful surrender. God knows that my every choice might just cause the vibrancy of those colors to fade. On those less-than-stellar days, the canvas gets filled. But it's far from a masterpiece. And yet, when the next day dawns, I am handed a canvas once more—proof that God's love really is deep. His grace really is sweet. His mercies really are brand-new. That stretched, stark-white canvas awaits my stroke. A masterpiece is ready to be born.

> *Heavenly Father, I pray for eyes that are open to seeing the brushstrokes of life—real life, life that is guided by You. I pray for ears to hear Your whispers as You lead. And I pray for a heart that beats only to the rhythm of Yours. Thank You for the potential masterpiece that is today.*

REFLECTION: Don't let a large canvas intimidate you. You can purchase one inexpensively, or just grab a sheet of paper. With a pen, colored pencils, or paints, create a picture of your present life. What do you see?

Journal, sketch, compose a poem, write a letter to God, meditate on a hymn or worship song that comes to mind.

Disappointed?

:: JILL SAVAGE ::

Jesus went out as usual to the Mount of Olives, and his disciples followed him. On reaching the place, he said to them, "Pray that you will not fall into temptation." He withdrew about a stone's throw beyond them, knelt down and prayed. . . . When he rose from prayer and went back to the disciples, he found them asleep . . . "Why are you sleeping?" he asked them.

LUKE 22:39–41, 45–46 NIV

Have you had a friend let you down? Has someone you love not followed through on a promise? We've all had people disappoint us at one time or another. But have you ever considered that Jesus also experienced disappointment when He lived on earth?

Sometimes we forget that Jesus was not only God on earth but also a human being. He experienced many of the same things that we experience. In these verses above, He asked His friends—the disciples—if they would pray with Him. He went off to pray and when He returned they were asleep. Can you imagine the disappointment Jesus must have felt? His friends let Him down.

Jesus not only understands disappointment, He also knows what it feels like to be tired, hungry, falsely accused, betrayed, and in pain. There's even a story in the Bible where Jesus and the disciples were in a boat when a storm blew in. The disciples were so scared they woke Jesus up in the middle of the night! That happens to me as a mom quite often when my children are scared in the night. Who would have thought that Jesus would understand interrupted sleep? But He does. When we face these everyday challenges, we're not alone. We have a God—a Friend—who truly understands.

Lord Jesus, thank You for setting the example for us to know how to live. But even more, thank You for coming to this earth as a human being. You understand the realities of life. Help me to remember that You are not a God who is far away and disconnected from my life, but You have experienced much of what I experience. Thank You for being a Friend who understands.

REFLECTION: What challenge are you facing that Jesus also experienced? As you read the Gospels, use your sacred imagination to see Jesus experiencing the hardship of humanity as you do.

Journal, sketch, compose a poem, write a letter to God, meditate on a hymn or worship song that comes to mind.

How Do I "Do Sad"?

:: SHELLY BEACH ::

He who sits on the throne said,
"Behold, I am making all things new." And He said,
"Write, for these words are faithful and true."

REVELATION 21:5 NASB

*T*oday I'll be hanging out with my friend Johnny who's visiting for a week with his mom, dad, and four brothers and sisters. He's just completed experimental treatment at St. Jude's Children's Hospital in Memphis and is visiting Michigan family and friends before heading home to Arkansas. The two hundred children each year who are diagnosed with Johnny's condition are considered terminal. Johnny's seven.

A friend recently asked me how I "do sad." As an author of caregiving books who walks beside people who are losing loved ones, and as an author of a book on self-talk, I appreciated the question. Grief and sadness can take us to despair, hopelessness, victimization, bitterness, and resentment.

But sadness and grief can also take us to God. In the book of Revelation, believers are given a picture of Jesus enthroned in heaven as He proclaims victory over sin and death and transforms all that was evil and hurtful in the world into something beautiful beyond what we can comprehend—the fulfillment of His final purposes.

When I'm taken to a place of sadness in my life, I walk through three simple steps in my self-talk:

S   Say what hurts. Express your pain to God. Grieve your losses.

A   Affirm the truth. Rest in God's character. Look at who God is and what He promises His children presently and for eternity.

D   Demonstrate praise and thanks. Live out what it means to trust a true and faithful God.

Sadness is part of living in a twisted world. Believers are called to "do sad" with the freedom to grieve our pain and losses but with the perspective of the source of our greater hope—Jesus Christ, who makes all things new.

> *Father God, may I learn each day what it means to bring my sadness to You, to affirm truth, and to rest in Your boundless love and provision for me. Help me to learn to live a life of worship that draws strength from You, even in my deepest pain. Amen.*

REFLECTION: How can you draw closer to God in the way you "do sad" in your life?

Journal, sketch, compose a poem, write a letter to God, meditate on a hymn or worship song that comes to mind.

Lonely but Not Alone

:: NANCY SEBASTIAN MEYER ::

And surely I am with you always,
to the very end of the age.

MATTHEW 28:20 NIV

T stood with the congregation, blinking rapidly to stop tears and unsuccessfully trying to get worship lyrics past the lump in my throat. My husband of eight years, a youth pastor for half that time, had just revealed his angst with God and subsequent defection from the faith. Sundays became the loneliest day of my week.

Months into this ordeal, I lay in bed beside my husband, trying to be free of anxious thoughts so I could sleep. Suddenly I sensed deep in my heart the very clear words, "Lo, I am with you always, even unto the end . . ." Peace, like a warm blanket straight out of the drier, enveloped my whole being. I recognized the words from a verse I had memorized in the King James Version as a child, but could not recall the reference. According to my request as I drifted off to sleep, God helped me find the verse in Matthew the next morning.

Normally I am a person who lives in the moment, in the present. I rarely get lonely or miss people, even on frequent trips away from home to speak at events. However, Sunday is a far different story as I sit alone in church, even when I remind myself that God is with me. Nineteen years have passed since Rich chose agnosticism. Still loneliness shrouds most Sundays—and spiritually single wives all over the world concur.

It comforts me to realize that loneliness was the one thing God pronounced "not good" during creation (Genesis 2:18). In the beginning He knew we would struggle with feelings of aloneness, at different times and in different ways. God graciously provides fellowship with other believers and comforting ties with family and friends. But best of all, He offers us the abiding presence of His Holy Spirit "to the very end of the age."

We may be lonely, but we are never alone.

> *I love You, O God, my Constant Companion, Husband, and Friend. In grateful adoration, I acknowledge Your presence here with me in this moment. I rest in the hollow of Your hand, Abba Father. Hallelujah!*

REFLECTION: How can you tangibly reach out to a lonely person today? What might that look like?

Journal, sketch, compose a poem, write a letter to God, meditate on a hymn or worship song that comes to mind.

Coming to Know the Freedom in Forgiveness

:: LORI NEFF ::

Bear with each other and forgive whatever
grievances you may have against one another.
Forgive as the Lord forgave you.

COLOSSIANS 3:13 NIV

I recently took a personality test for work. It confirmed much of what I already know—I tend to be goal-oriented, introverted, independent, persistent. It also showed me some of my flaws right there in black-and-white . . . not so fun. It told me that I can tend to be too blunt and indecisive, and that I hold grudges. Painful to read, but I have to admit that it's true. In fact, I've seen the ugly "grudge" descriptor pop up in past test results. That test got me thinking about forgiveness.

I recently met with MBI professor and occasional *Midday Connection* guest Nancy Kane. During a meeting over hot cups of tea, I mentioned a grudge that I was having a hard time letting go of. I know in my head that holding on to the hurt only harms me (like the old saying that says bitterness is like me drinking poison, hoping the other person gets sick!). As I talked with her, I realized that I wanted the other person to hurt as much as they hurt me and if I let the grudge go, it would be like letting them get away with it.

I know that God says that He will take care of vengeance, but I wanted vengeance sooner rather than later! She told me that a key in forgiveness might just be remembering my sin is just as big as the other person's. The other person's sin was visible and the damage caused was immediately tangible. My own sin is just less visible and the damage might be subtle and not seen right away. Knowing my own need for forgiveness and having the right view of God's grace will surely compel me to forgive others. God is still working in my life (thankfully, He never gives up on me!) and I'm getting closer to forgiving. I'm thankful for friends who can speak truth in love to help me grow more like Christ and be the woman He created me to be . . . forgiving and free.

Loving God, teach me about the freedom that comes with forgiveness.

REFLECTION: Is God nudging you to forgive someone? What's holding you back?

Journal, sketch, compose a poem, write a letter to God, meditate on a hymn or worship song that comes to mind.

What's True?

:: MARILYN HONTZ ::

Keep me from lying to myself.
PSALM 119:29 NLT

*H*ave you ever stood in front of a mirror and felt disgusted by what you saw? Recently I was getting ready to go shopping with my daughter, Abby. After running a brush through my hair, I took a quick glance in the bathroom mirror and remarked, "Ugh, my hair looks awful!" Abby quickly responded, "No, Mom, your hair looks fine!" Now, who was I going to believe?

It was helpful to have my daughter there to correct my faulty thinking because the mirror was not going to say to me, "You, my dear, are the fairest of them all!" Many times, however, what we see in the mirror has nothing to do with hair but rather with feelings of inadequacy. We forget that we have Someone who *is* standing next to us as we look at ourselves. It is the Lord Jesus. He whispers, *I love you, you are beautiful in My eyes; you are My beloved child. Please believe Me! Do not lie to yourself—even as you seek not to lie to others, do not pick up the addicting habit of lying to yourself. To do so immobilizes you and keeps you from accomplishing the works I have ordained for you to do.*

> *Dearest Father, it's easy to slip into the lies I believe about myself. I ask that Your Holy Spirit would convict me when I do this—just as You would convict me if I had lied to someone else. Help me replace the lies I believe about myself with truth from Your Word. Satan knows that if I could grasp the truth that You love me—nothing would hold me back from partnering with You to have an impact on earth and eternity. Please help me to have an honest estimate of myself, based on Your truth, so I am free to serve You instead of feeling unworthy or inadequate. And remind me often that I am made in Your image. In Jesus' name, AMEN!*

REFLECTION: Whose words are you going to believe—your thoughts or God's Word? You have a choice! The verse "Keep me from lying to myself . . ." goes on to say, "Give me the privilege of knowing your instructions." Are you willing to know and accept God's evaluation of you?

Journal, sketch, compose a poem, write a letter to God, meditate on a hymn or worship song that comes to mind.

How Beautiful!

:: JANE RUBIETTA ::

*Let everything that has breath
praise the Lord. Praise the Lord.*

PSALM 150:6 NIV

hough some people, John Wesley among them, say,
"Cleanliness is next to godliness" (it's not in the Scriptures, in case you look), very few jobs around the
house float my boat. Just being honest. I'm not a fan of cleaning just because cleaning is necessary. Especially when ten
minutes or ten hours or ten days later, the work needs repeat-
ing. But that's not even why I don't love doing most of the
tasks. Deep down, it's because maybe no one notices.

Selfish? Maybe. Low self-worth? Maybe. Realistic? Yes. Not
that I clean for others' approval, but when I finally do clean,
it's out of love for them. That and/or because company is coming. Maybe it seems unspiritual, ungodly of me. (Insert shrug
of shoulders here, and wide eyes.)

For me, one means of staying in more constant contact
with God (since God doesn't send out e-letters) has been

noticing. Noticing the elm tree outside, with its six million leaves waving at me. Noticing how the sun bounces off the plate-glass water in the morning. One night, on a short almost-country walk with my husband, we kept hearing a shushing-rustling sound. An animal, maybe? Finally, I grabbed Rich's arm and braked. "Shh. Listen."

We stood stock-still beside acres of corn. The wind tickled the drying leaves and husks, jiggling the stalks. The entire field sang a soft lullaby! We listened for several minutes, and then I said, almost breathless, "Thank You, God. How beautiful."

Imagine all the creative work God goes to, since eternity past and forever, to please us. I think God loves it when we notice, and smile, and say "Thank You." Because it really is one of the ways He loves us.

I feel challenged to go attack some cobwebs. They really are amazing. And even if no one notices, I can notice, and say "Thank You." And . . . I think I feel a smile coming on.

> *God, You are amazing. Your love shows up every-*
> *where. Thank You! Help me to notice Your handi-*
> *work, to be drawn into Your presence, and to love*
> *others through both handiwork . . . and noticing.*

REFLECTION: Where do you notice God's love for you? How can you notice it, even more? What difference does it make?

Journal, sketch, compose a poem, write a letter to God,
meditate on a hymn or worship song that comes to mind.

Red Light

:: DAWN HERZOG JEWELL ::

I am fearfully and wonderfully made.
PSALM 139:14 NIV

Three years ago, God was knitting together our first child in my womb. Thinking we might have a girl, my husband and I named the growing baby "Lucy."

In early May, during my second trimester, I kissed my husband good-bye and boarded a plane for Europe to research for my book about God's work in red-light districts. I would trek inside brothels and down seedy alleys to learn how Jesus' followers were befriending prostituting women and men.

On a drizzly Monday night in Amsterdam's historic red-light district, I walk cobblestone streets past brothel windows displaying women posing in lacy lingerie. I am trailing Toos Heemskerk, a vivacious Dutch woman with Scharlaken Koord (Scarlet Cord) who leads weekly visits to these women from dozens of countries.

A young girl opens the first glass door Toos knocks on.

116

Her freckled face and brown eyes bear no makeup, and she is wearing a modest white swimsuit. She looks sixteen, and like any girl in my neighborhood. Toos introduces herself and inquires where she is from. "Hungary." Her name is Lucy.

Instantly, God shook my comfortable world: *She could be your daughter.*

When Lucy was a little girl, I'm sure she never dreamed of selling her body to strange men in a foreign city, far from home. In a slow economy, perhaps she was deceived by an ad to waitress or nanny abroad, then forced to submit to a violent pimp. Or, maybe Lucy was desperate to pay hospital bills for her ailing mother and support siblings back home.

Millions of women and girls like Lucy, and even boys and men, are sexually exploited around the world every day in brothels, strip clubs, massage parlors, karaoke bars, dark alleys, and false storefronts. Many give up hope for a life of dignity. But like the son I gave birth to, they are "fearfully and wonderfully made."

> *Lord, please shake Your church, raise up Your people to extend hands of hope and friendship to these wounded girls, women, boys, and men. They need to know that they are Your beloved children.*

IN PLACE of a reflection today, *Midday Connection* recommends reading Dawn's book *Escaping the Devil's Bedroom: Sex Trafficking, Global Prostitution, and the Gospel's Transforming Power.*

Journal, sketch, compose a poem, write a letter to God, meditate on a hymn or worship song that comes to mind.

Misplaced?

:: LEIGH McLEROY ::

*He who has found his life will lose it,
and he who has lost his life for My sake will find it.*

MATTHEW 10:39 NASB

Recently I ordered a diet Dr. Pepper at a fast-food drive-through, and the voice of the order-taker chirped, "It's a great day at _____. What can we make for you today?" I know they didn't "make" my soda for me, but for a moment I felt special because I want what I want, when and how I want it, and my order-taker recognized that.

Truthfully, I am seldom unaware of my wants or of how the fulfillment of a few of them might inconvenience (or even hurt) others. Only by giving free rein to the Spirit of God in me do I effectively defeat my inherent selfishness. Only by saying yes to Christ am I able to shush the clamor of my own interests. And the world offers no help, because the world tells me that it is perfectly fine to worship in the "temple of me."

Advertising insists every want of mine is legitimate, and

immediately obtainable. Even billboards for places of God-worship hint at who they really aim to please: "You'll love it," they promise of their church, or "There's a place for you." But how difficult is it to make the necessary switch of focus when those who are told it's all about them learn there's only One who rightly deserves the place of highest honor.

Pastor/poet George Herbert, in his collection of poems called *The Temple*, wrote these words: "O what man would be, if he could himself misplace!" If we could misplace or lose ourselves, we would be found. Jesus said that. The Spirit calls us to that. The Father is glorified by that. But the world won't help dismantle my self-styled temple of me. Only the desire to live for Jesus' sake can do that. Because the temple is His, not mine.

> *Father, I do want Your interests to supersede my own. Please help me to "misplace" myself so that Your will might be done not just "on earth as it is in heaven" but in my life, today.*

REFLECTION: Where is your true worship focused? What self-interests keep you from fully following the Lord Jesus Christ and being found in Him?

Journal, sketch, compose a poem, write a letter to God, meditate on a hymn or worship song that comes to mind.

Wise Woman

:: MARCIA RAMSLAND ::

The wise woman builds her house . . .
PROVERBS 14:1 NIV

I often speak to women's groups and find they want to hear about one life issue: How can I get organized so I have more time? Ironically I know if they do get organized, they will get more done but not necessarily have more time. Why? Because we women often lose focus on the purpose behind all our activities.

Having a purpose and not just a time-driven life came home to me last summer after the wedding of our last child. I was happy Christy, Lisa, and Mark were all married with spouses, homes, and careers of their own. But it was the end of thirty-one years of parenting for me. No more meals to cook for more than my husband and me. No more scheduling around the myriad of children's events. No more stress of getting everyone out the door in the morning.

I had time, but I had to find a new purpose. My focus had been Proverbs 14:1 to be "the wise woman building my house." We built harmony, goals, and vision into our children. My father had given me that purpose by saying, "You don't know the results of your parenting until you see your grand-children." He set my sights long-range to build my home to see godly children growing up and creating their own fami-lies. It worked to lift my sights beyond laundry, pickup, car pooling, and waiting until they left home.

Today I share with you a plaque that sits in my home that also gave me focus. "Home . . .Where each lives for the other and all live for God."

You may want to post that in your kitchen or frame it to hang on the wall in the family room. It's a reminder that the WISE woman builds her house, and that's a worthy focus that will give you more time in your day!

> *Dear Lord, thank You for creating us as women who are able to multitask—able to take care of work, family, singleness, and whatever life brings our way with Your presence. Whatever our circumstance today, give us insight to build into the people in our world so they love You and desire to go deeper with You. Amen.*

REFLECTION: How can you build into those in your home and life today?

Journal, sketch, compose a poem, write a letter to God, meditate on a hymn or worship song that comes to mind.

Be Bold

:: CHRISTA MARCH ::

*So let us come boldly to the throne of our gracious
God. There we will receive his mercy, and we will find
grace to help us when we need it most.*

HEBREWS 4:16 NLT

Several years ago I spent the summer in Germany. During
my time there I visited vineyards, saw historical sites,
and toured castles. It was during one castle tour that my
prayer life changed.

Castle Schwerin was not just a castle; it was a palace!
Every room inside had been refashioned to look just as it had
in the sixteenth century. The furnishings were made of the
best woods, precious stones, and gold.

The last room we entered was the Throne Room. It took
two tour guides to open the heavy doors. When the doors
opened our entire group, together as one person, gasped. The
room was stunning, truly fit for a king! Beautiful stained-glass
windows on both sides of the room showered the room with
light and color. A long red carpet ran from the doors right up

to the throne. The throne itself was pure gold embedded with jewels. *This must be what the throne room of heaven looks like!* I thought. Then I began to wonder about the other people who came into this throne room hundreds of years ago. I could picture the "commoners" slowly, fearfully approaching the throne afraid of what the mighty king might say or do to them.

Our heavenly King opens His throne room and instructs us to "come boldly to the throne." When we approach His throne, He promises that we will find mercy and grace when we need it the most. How blessed we are to know that when we pray, we are entering into the throne room of the most gracious King of kings and Lord of lords!

> *Most High King, Ruler of my heart and the universe,*
> *thank You for sending Your Son to pay the penalty*
> *for my sin so I can boldly enter Your throne room.*
> *Thank You for being a loving, compassionate King*
> *who promises me mercy and grace when I need it*
> *the most.*

REFLECTION: Draw a picture of a throne. Picture yourself standing before it in God's presence. Are you intimidated? Are you sensing His love, mercy, and grace?

Journal, sketch, compose a poem, write a letter to God,
meditate on a hymn or worship song that comes to mind.

Look Around

:: KAY YERKOVICH ::

*Behold, he passes by me, and I see him not; he moves
on, but I do not perceive him. If I summoned him and
he answered me, I would not believe that he was listening to my voice. For he crushes me with a tempest
and multiplies my wounds without cause; he will not
let me get my breath, but fills me with bitterness.*

JOB 9:11, 16–18 ESV

I heard a sermon about "tapping into the presence of
God" as the solution to making it through difficult
times. Just get cozy with Jesus and all will be well.
After thirty-eight years of walking with the Lord, I don't think
it's quite that easy or formulaic. God is always present. Per-
ceiving God's presence is another matter entirely. Sometimes
God mercifully gives us a distinct awareness of His company,
love, and care. Other times, we know it only by faith. During
the most challenging seasons, we feel like Job; God has turned
His back and we suffer alone. Prayers hit the ceiling. The Bible
reading is dry. We long for a touch from God, but no touch
comes. Job's honesty is solace for a struggling sojourner.

Job reveals his feelings during his agonizing labor, which finally gives birth to resting in the power and mystery of God Himself as revealed in creation. Romans 1:20 says that God's invisible attributes, power, and divine nature, are demonstrated in the body you inhabit and the world outside your front door. God's answer? "Look around, Job." Job's response? "I lay my hand on my mouth." When we realize His ways are beyond understanding, our view of God is enlarged and we are speechless.

Lord, we live with proof of Your presence in every leaf, flower, and blade of grass. We marvel at the magnificence of Your creation from a tiny cell to the farthest star. May we put our hand on our mouth and stand in awe of Your glorious power. Sometimes You withhold Your power and allow our suffering to continue. May we remember what the suffering of Christ accomplished and trust we do not suffer in vain but within the purpose of Your love even when the reason remains a mystery.

REFLECTION: How can you enlarge your vision of God? Sometime soon look for the largeness of God in creation.

Journal, sketch, compose a poem, write a letter to God, meditate on a hymn or worship song that comes to mind.

Begin Again

:: SHARON HERSH ::

He who was seated on the throne said,
"I am making everything new!"

REVELATION 21:5 NIV

What is the first thing you thought about this morning? Prayed about last night? Worried about throughout the day? I imagine if we could have a face-to-face conversation about what you think about, dream for, persistently pray about, risk for over and over again, discuss with your friends, are willing to look like a fool for, and continually hope for *more* in, we would see your heart for relationships.

God created us to long for purposeful, passionate, mutual relationships and yet we all have stories of heartache when relationships falter.

St. Frances de Sales wrote, "There is no better way to attain the spiritual life than by beginning again." Beginning again can seem overwhelming when our dreams have been shattered, our plans thwarted, and our hearts broken. Beginning again often starts with something simple . . .

I tell my parents, my children, and my friends what I love about them.

I call a friend I haven't talked to for weeks, confronting my own shame at allowing the friendship to lapse, and discover that she's been feeling the same way.

I say "Thank You" for all the gifts in my life.

I listen with expectant hope to love songs on the radio.

I restart the journal I began last fall with a commitment to record evidence of God's care for me every day.

One of my favorite artists, Brian Andreas, wrote, "Anyone can slay dragons, but waking up every morning and loving the world all over again . . . That's what takes a real hero." It takes courage to begin again and believe again even though our relationships have brought failure, brokenness, fractured families, addiction, abuse, judgment, and shattered dreams. God gave us a heart for relationships because waking up every morning and beginning again, believing again, forgiving again, risking again, and dwelling in the possibilities again—that takes a real hero.

God, give me the courage to begin again.

REFLECTION: Write out a list of your "begin agains."

Journal, sketch, compose a poem, write a letter to God, meditate on a hymn or worship song that comes to mind.

Sanctuary

:: JOANNE FAIRCHILD MILLER ::

A heart at peace gives life to the body.
PROVERBS 14:30 NIV

Long ago my husband and I determined to create a haven of peace in our home after watching the old version of *The Hunchback of Notre Dame*. Quasimodo would retreat to the safety of the church, yell "Sanctuary!" and be assured that no harm would come to him while under that roof.

In creating a sanctuary in our home, I incorporated all the senses to construct a safe place to protect our family from outside negative influences. When my children came home from school, they were often greeted with the smell of freshly baked bread or cookies. My husband came home to thirty minutes of solitude in a hot tub of water with the flicker of candlelight and soft music before we bombarded him with tales of our daily adventures. No one had a television in their bedroom. When we sat down to watch a movie, we did it as a family. During the week, in lieu of television, we listened to good music while eating meals together; we played board games, and we laughed at the stories and tales each of us had to share. Our finances were meager but we created fond memories of time spent laughing and celebrating peace within the walls of our home.

We developed a family mission statement together that helped eliminate arguing, power struggles, jealousy, and anger. Our common goal was to maintain peace within our home regardless of what happened in the world around us.

Often our friends comment on the peaceful atmosphere as they enter our home, and it is comforting to see our married children carrying on the same tradition and creating peace within their homes in spite of a world full of war and chaos.

Lord, You are the Prince of Peace. Help me to refrain from sin that creates disharmony in my soul. Help me to create a sanctuary where my loved ones and friends can come for renewal and rest and know they have had time spent with You because only You can fill us with perfect peace that passes all understanding.

REFLECTION: What are you doing to make your home a sanctuary of peace for friends and family?

Journal, sketch, compose a poem, write a letter to God, meditate on a hymn or worship song that comes to mind.

Talking to Jesus

:: MINDY CALIGUIRE ::

*"Lord, teach us to pray, just as John taught his
disciples." He said to them, "When you pray, say:
'Father, hallowed be your name, your kingdom come.
Give us each day our daily bread. Forgive us our sins,
for we also forgive everyone who sins against us.
And lead us not into temptation.'"*

LUKE 11:1–4 NIV

*D*o you ever wonder what you would ask Jesus if He were right here with you in person—right there, standing next to you—just as He was with those original disciples?

I do. Often. To be clear, that's not stopping me from praying on many occasions for many reasons . . . but I still find there are times I have questions. Hard questions. Scary questions. Questions that I'd like to ask while looking into His eyes to see His response as much as *hear* it.

But would I have had the wisdom to ask Jesus what His original followers asked Him? Would I have wanted to know how to pray? I hope so. Maybe that simple question is at the heart of my desire to connect so directly.

Over the past few years, I have discovered something about Jesus' answer: it was good advice. At the risk of sounding outrageous, here's what I mean. Of all the many ways of prayer I've learned over the years, and grown significantly through, I often find myself returning to Jesus' famous answer to that simple, sincere question.

One of the many gifts His prayer offers is a structure, or a framework, to guide me as I take each portion and personalize it to the day's concerns or activities. Here are a few questions that can help you do the same:

What's one thing you really appreciate about God's greatness?
In what way do you look forward to God's ways triumphing?
What's a current, tangible need you have in your life today?
What's one thing you need forgiveness for right now?
Who is one person who has wounded you recently, in large or small ways?
What could easily pull you away from God?

Now take a few minutes and pray through the Lord's Prayer again, using your own words.

Lord, teach us to pray.

REFLECTION: What one or two questions from the list above can you take with you and pray about over the course of today?

Journal, sketch, compose a poem, write a letter to God, meditate on a hymn or worship song that comes to mind.

Lying to Ourselves

:: JENNIFER DEGLER ::

*Instead, speaking the truth in love, we will in all things
grow up into him who is the Head, that is, Christ.*

EPHESIANS 4:15 NIV

*J*esus spoke the truth in love in every situation regardless of what it cost Him. If you want to grow up into the full image of Christ, then you also must be a truth speaker—and that starts with speaking the truth to yourself. Often the person we lie to the most is ourselves. Why? Because lies protect us temporarily from facing painful truths. The truth can hurt, but the truth, spoken in love, does not permanently harm us or anyone else. It's like going to your dentist. She may hurt you, but she's not harming you. The pain you feel is actually helping you become healthier.

Where are you lying to yourself? Perhaps you are accepting verbal, physical, financial, sexual, spiritual, or emotional abuse and telling yourself "this is not abuse." Maybe you are trying to convince yourself that your unhealthy relationships aren't harming you or your family. Possibly you are denying

132

how dangerous the long-term consequences are for the poor choices you are making. Whatever the lie, it's time to grow up, and speak the truth, the whole truth, and nothing but the truth—first to yourself and then to others.

Yes, the truth often hurts, but it's also the first step toward freedom. In John 8, Jesus said, "The truth will set you free." The reverse is true as well: "Lies will imprison you"—imprison you in unhealthy and possibly dangerous relationships and behavior patterns. Becoming a truth speaker like Jesus will open the doors to freedom.

Heavenly Father, show me where I may be lying to myself. Please speak truth into my life and help me to grow from the pain this may cause me. When I am tempted today to deny or hide from the truth, remind me that accepting the truth will keep me free. Strengthen my courage and resolve so that I speak the truth in love in all situations no matter the cost, just as Jesus did.

REFLECTION: What truths do I need to speak about my relationships? My choices? My actions? How would my life be different if I spoke those truths in love to myself? To others?

Journal, sketch, compose a poem, write a letter to God, meditate on a hymn or worship song that comes to mind.

When There Are No Words

:: MONA SHRIVER ::

Three times I pleaded with the Lord to take it away
from me. But he said to me, "My grace is sufficient for
you, for my power is made perfect in weakness."

2 CORINTHIANS 12:8–9 NIV

I'd spent the past three years studying God's Word and growing in my faith. My husband had spent that same time in an adulterous relationship. I was angry and confused. It wasn't fair. As the shock faded and reality sunk in, I felt the only solution would be to wake from this nightmare. I even dreamed I'd wake up. In my dream, I'd awakened in the hospital and saw my husband and his affair partner standing together at my bedside. When I told them they couldn't be there together and why, they said the words I longed to hear: "It never happened. You've been sick and only dreamed it." For a few brief moments in the twilight of awakening, I believed. Then as the light of day reached my eyes, I remembered. It had happened. My best friend and my husband had betrayed me.

134

I, like Paul, wanted it to be taken away. No good could come of this sin. My marriage was in shambles, my God dishonored.

I felt helpless and alone. I saw only shame.

As we tried to work our way through the maze of sin and its consequences, I watched myself succumb to overwhelming devastation. I feared I would not survive.

In one of my darkest moments, my legs gave way beneath me and I slid to the floor in total and absolute weakness. Then I heard God's quiet whisper tell me I'd be okay. I would survive. For the first time I understood what Paul meant when he said God's grace was sufficient. I wanted my marriage to be saved but whether it was or not, I would survive.

I didn't have a clue what my life would look like in the future, but God's power would get me through. I received strength to stand one more time.

Thank You, Father, that Your grace is enough and
Your power sends light through the darkness.

REFLECTION: When there are no words, sometimes an artistic expression helps to open our hearts. Consider making a collage to express your pain and hurt. Use your art to lift a prayer to God.

Journal, sketch, compose a poem, write a letter to God,
meditate on a hymn or worship song that comes to mind.

Being Seen

:: CARYN RIVADENEIRA ::

The angel of the Lord also said to [Hagar],
"You are now with child and you will have a son.
You shall name him Ishmael, for the
Lord has heard of your misery. . . .

[Hagar] gave this name to the Lord who spoke to her:
"You are the God who sees me," for she said,
"I now have seen the One who sees me."

GENESIS 16:11, 13 NIV

To say that I can relate to Hagar would be the overstatement of the year. I've never been a slave. I've never been "given" to my boss so I could have his baby. I've never been so mistreated by someone that I'd rather run away to die in the desert than to stay another day with her. Frankly, there's little about Hagar's horror-story-of-a-life that lines up with mine.

And yet, when I read this passage where the angel names Hagar's son Ishmael (which means, "God hears") and when Hagar names God, *El Roi* ("The One who sees me"), I feel a kinship with her. I wish I could hug her. Because I too have had that moment with God where I—in the midst of my own deep pain, huge fear, and major confusion—understood that God hears me and God sees me.

If you've experienced it, then you know it's a moment that changes everything about our lives.

Of course knowing that God sees and hears doesn't mean that we get a pass from the difficulties of life. Hagar sure didn't. Neither have I.

While we may not understand what God is doing, what we've been through, what we're going through now, or what we're being called to do, knowing that God sees, hears, and is with us (Emmanuel!) gives us hope and courage to face whatever comes.

> *Thank You for hearing our giggles and our cries. For seeing our successes and our failures. Thank You for loving us and for walking with us through them all. Help us remember that—like Hagar—our job is not to understand Your ways, but to follow them, faithfully, with the hope and faith that comes from knowing You see and You hear. Amen.*

REFLECTION: When have you known God's presence in your journey? What is an image that represents God's presence with you?

Journal, sketch, compose a poem, write a letter to God, meditate on a hymn or worship song that comes to mind.

Tending the Soul

SECTION THREE

Being Myself

:: LORI NEFF ::

We have different gifts, according to the grace given us.
ROMANS 12:6 NIV

One of my goals this year was to get involved in a younger woman's life. Sounds like a good goal, right? Well, honestly, the thought of it scared me to death. What would I have to offer to a younger woman? But even though I felt afraid, I knew that this was something that I should do and really did want to do.

Looking at my overly full schedule, I held my breath as I signed up for a mentoring program at work. I was soon matched up with a college sophomore named Alexis. I had a stomachache and sweaty palms as I went to meet her for the first time! After our first few visits, while I enjoyed our conversations, I felt like a failure. I didn't have any good answers for her questions. After agonizing and praying, I realized that I was trying to be someone I'm not. God intended that I bring *me* to the relationship—the woman He made me to be. I'm a listener and I love to ask questions. I don't often give advice, but I love to help people think through things. That gave me such a peace (and relief that I didn't have to have all the answers!).

I can relax now and just be myself—and that enriches our relationship. As we've gotten to know each other, it's become so clear that God brought us together. It's been challenging and fun to be involved with a vibrant, expressive, intelligent young woman. We've known each other for only a few months, but that time has been full of hot tea, tears, hugs, prayer, overnights, shared meals, and lots of laughter. I have come to love her very much and am so thankful for her and how my life is more beautiful with her in it.

> *Lord, please show me how to bring myself—gifts,*
> *personality, and abilities that You've given to me—*
> *to the world around me.*

REFLECTION: In what area of your life do you feel that you could bring more of yourself? What's holding you back?

Journal, sketch, compose a poem, write a letter to God,
meditate on a hymn or worship song that comes to mind.

Taking Steps toward Healing

:: VICTORIA SAUNDERS JOHNSON ::

*"But I will restore you to health and
heal your wounds," declares the Lord.*

JEREMIAH 30:17 NIV

Linda was about twelve when her father began molesting her. "Twenty-six years have passed," she says, "but the pain and confusion are as fresh as if it were yesterday." Linda was determined to rid her mind and heart of past issues before she reached her fortieth birthday. "I no longer want to keep questioning God, blaming my mother, and wallowing in bitterness and self-pity."

Linda's spiritual mom, Mother Green who had suffered a similar experience, assured her, "God is able, Linda. He can set you free. I'm a living witness."

"How?" Linda asked.

"The first step is admitting and talking about what happened." Linda dropped her head. "I know, this is very hard," Mother Green said as she rocked Linda as though she were a little girl. "All the anger and fear comes flooding

142

back. But you've got to admit the truth."

Over the next few months, Mother Green and Linda talked and prayed together. "Linda, seek Him, He's your *Jehovah Rapha*. He can take the bitter waters of your life and make them sweet. He's our Great Physician. The abuse shattered you inside, but He can make you whole."

Gradually, Linda learned how to pour out her heart. As waves of emotion washed over her—good and bad—she imagined herself releasing them all at the cross of Jesus Christ. His cleansing blood covered her shame. She experienced His unfailing, unconditional love. She also memorized Scriptures that enabled her to reprogram negative, damaging thoughts. Mother Green challenged her to begin the process of forgiving the offender and family members who knew about her pain, yet had remained silent.

Linda threw a huge fortieth birthday party. In the middle of the celebration, she bravely stood up and shared her entire story. She emphasized the faithfulness of God who helped her overcome the abuse, and made a commitment to help others. When she finished, Mother Green was the first one on her feet as the room erupted in clapping, crying, and a standing ovation.

Yes, Lord, I am ready. I believe You are my Great Physician and able to heal me from the inside out.

REFLECTION: God is willing; are you? What are your first steps? Can you identify a Mother Green in your life?

Journal, sketch, compose a poem, write a letter to God, meditate on a hymn or worship song that comes to mind.

Helping the Ones We Love

:: ANN SPANGLER ::

Christ in you, the hope of glory.
COLOSSIANS 1:27 NIV

I yelled at my daughter today. The words came blasting out like water from a fire hose.

Friends say I pray well. I'm articulate. Truth be told, I shout well too.

My angry comments pelted down on her. *Lazy, insubordinate, inconsiderate, selfish, insensitive.* How would she like it, I said, if I were to stop taking care of her for a week? She could cook her own meals, pay her own tuition, buy her food, do her laundry, and clean the house. Maybe then she would appreciate all the wonderful, selfless, kind things I do for her every single day of her life. The words continued in a great torrent, berating, biting, criticizing, correcting.

Afterward, the obvious truth hit me. Words like these, spoken in anger, will never move my child's heart in a good direction. No matter how much I want her to change, she will not be touched and transformed by my frustration but only by the energy of Christ expressed through me.

How do we help the people we love? So often we pressure them with good ideas or words designed to shake and change them. But it never works. After a while, we feel anguish, unable to find a solution to their problems. Answers emerge, Larry Crabb says in his book *Connecting*, when we finally "face the truth that a troubled, hardened, foolish heart needs to be impacted and that only the Spirit of God can make that happen." As we seek God, "we will land on the truth of his eternal, almighty, and loving character, and we will believe he is always up to something good. And we will find him within us in the form of holy urges and good appetites and wise inclinations that reflect the character of Christ.

"In more familiar language, the energy of Christ is released most fully when we most completely come to an end of ourselves."

> *Lord, nothing I say or do can change another person's heart. Only the energy of Your life at work within me can do that. Live and speak and act in me for the sake of Your glory, I pray.*

REFLECTION: How might your relationships be transformed if you were to let Christ step forward in your reactions to others?

Journal, sketch, compose a poem, write a letter to God, meditate on a hymn or worship song that comes to mind.

What Are You Thinking About?

:: STASI ELDREDGE ::

Whatever is true, whatever is noble, whatever is right, whatever is pure, whatever is lovely, whatever is admirable—if anything is excellent or praiseworthy—think about such things.

PHILIPPIANS 4:8 NIV

I woke this morning feeling braced for my day. It's a pretty day, but a pretty full day. A very full day. It's too full! My thoughts began to spiral downward with a life of their own. Panic was beginning to set in and I hadn't even brushed my teeth yet. How in the world can I get everything done today that needs my attention *and* be a loving woman in the midst of it?! It's too much to ask of a person.

Well, truly, it is too much to ask of a person. But it's not too much to ask of Jesus. The good news that God reminded me of this morning is that I can't do anything worth doing without Him and *I am not* without Him. I am not living my life by myself, alone.

The Holy Spirit is right here, right now, dwelling inside me. I have the life of Christ living in me and through me. And

Jesus cares. He cares about every aspect of my life. And every aspect of your life. He cares deeply. He's that good!

What a relief to turn my thoughts to the One who is true, noble, right, pure, lovely, admirable, excellent, and praiseworthy! Jesus is my ever present help and so I can choose not to panic but to worship.

> *Dear Jesus, thank You for the gift of this new day. I invite You into it and into me. Again. I choose at this moment to fix the gaze of my heart and my thoughts on who You are, and I ask for Your strength and grace to fill me today. Live through me, Jesus. Help me to accomplish that which needs to be accomplished, and help me to remember that You are God. You are good. You are my strength. You are with me. And You are more than enough. In Your name, I pray. Amen*

REFLECTION: What circumstance or relationship is feeling too much for you today? Invite God into it.

Journal, sketch, compose a poem, write a letter to God, meditate on a hymn or worship song that comes to mind.

Rejoicing Always

:: MARGARET MANNING ::

Rejoice always, pray without ceasing,
give thanks in all circumstances; for this is
the will of God in Christ Jesus for you.

1 THESSALONIANS 5:16–18 ESV

*C*hristians spend a good deal of time wondering about the will of God for their lives. Should I take that other job? Do we move across the country? Is this the man I should marry? Sometimes in worrying about finding God's will in the specific details of our lives, we miss the clear presentation from Scripture concerning God's will. The apostle Paul tells the Thessalonian Christians that the will of God in Christ Jesus for them is to "rejoice always, pray constantly, and give thanks in all circumstances"!

No one ever said God's will would be easy. Giving thanks in all circumstances seems a difficult demand when things are bad. Yet, this command is joined with the exhortation to pray constantly and prayers are often filled with lament and sorrow—just read the prayers of the psalmists.

148

We can "rejoice always" as we entrust our lives to the God who is "working all things together for our good," and who desires to conform us to the image of Christ. When we remember that some of the deepest expressions of gratitude in Scripture come from those who experienced the darkest of times, we understand that this aspect of God's will does not mean we will always feel happy, or feel like rejoicing. Rather, the rejoicing and the thanksgiving arise out of a heart that trusts in the Lord who has saved us, and who is faithful to save us no matter what our circumstances. As Paul concludes his letter to the Thessalonians, he reminds them about why they can rejoice and be thankful: "He who calls you is faithful; he will surely do it" (5:24).

Lord God, thank You for revealing Your will to us in Christ Jesus. Help me, this day, to rejoice, pray, and give thanks to You in all my unique circumstances.

REFLECTION: Find a three-minute window in your day when you can be alone. Ask God to speak to you. Spend some time playing worship music and let it wash over you. Can you worship God even in your pain, being thankful for who He is?

Journal, sketch, compose a poem, write a letter to God, meditate on a hymn or worship song that comes to mind.

In a Minute

:: KENDRA SMILEY ::

The law of the Lord is perfect, reviving the soul.
The statutes of the Lord are trustworthy, making wise
the simple. The precepts of the Lord are right, giving
joy to the heart. The commands of the Lord are radi-
ant, giving light to the eyes. The fear of the Lord is
pure, enduring forever. The ordinances of the Lord
are sure and altogether righteous.

PSALM 19:7–9 NIV

I am the youngest of my parents' three children. I have a brother twelve years my senior and a sister ten years older. According to my siblings, one of my favorite words as a preschooler was "inaminit." You have probably already guessed that "inaminit" is a combination of three words: in a minute.

"Kendra, it's time to put away your toys." "Inaminit!"

"Please help me find your shoes." "Inaminit!"

"Go wash your hands for dinner." "Inaminit!"

I was never overtly disagreeing or refusing to cooperate. I was, however, trying to control when I chose to comply with the instruction. As I recall, my one word response was not too effective and eventually it was retired.

It is likely I have never actually told the Lord, "Inaminit," but I have to admit I have not always been immediately obedient to His Word. All too often I have read His instruction and chosen to comply at a later time.

When I reflect on the Scripture above, I am reminded that His law is perfect, His statues are trustworthy, and His precepts are right and joy giving. Those words encourage me to be obedient to the instruction in His Word in a more timely manner. If I am wise, I will not reply with "inaminit" when it comes to His commands and ordinances. I will see to it that "inaminit" does not come out of retirement!

> *Dear Heavenly Father, thank You for Your Word.*
> *Thank You for Your instructions that are pure and*
> *lead to right living. I love You and desire to obey*
> *Your commands. Thank You for equipping me to be*
> *obedient. Please forgive me for those times I have*
> *been slow to obey.*

REFLECTION: Have you ever told the Lord "inaminit" when He has given you an instruction? What is it that He is asking you to do and why are you hesitant to follow through?

Journal, sketch, compose a poem, write a letter to God,
meditate on a hymn or worship song that comes to mind.

Seen by God

:: CAROLYN CUSTIS JAMES ::

You are the God who sees me.
GENESIS 16:13 NIV

Among all the women in the Bible whose stories I've written about in my books, Hagar the Egyptian slave girl draws the most comments by far from readers. Historically, Hagar's claim to fame is that she is the mother of Ishmael, Abraham's son. But while her story was playing out, she had no claim to fame and was, in fact, a secondary character living inside other people's stories.

With the powerlessness of a relay baton, Hagar is handed off by Pharaoh to appease an offended Abraham, who passes her on to serve barren Sarah, who hands her back to childless Abraham to bear a son. The scheme was perfectly acceptable in the ancient culture. Today, we call it trafficking.

The part of Hagar's story that hits a nerve with so many readers comes when a pregnant Hagar unwisely exults over the infertile Sarah, provoking outrage and abuse. Frightened and distraught, Hagar flees into the wilderness where the

Angel of the Lord pursues her, speaks her name (something neither Sarah nor Abraham do), asks what is going on with her, and pulls her into His story.

Overwhelmed, Hagar names the Angel *El Roi,* saying, "You are the God who sees me." Hagar may be invisible to everyone else. She is neon bright on God's radar. It is a watershed moment for Hagar.

But God does more than reassure. He gives Hagar a mission, for she is God's image bearer. That means she has kingdom work to do. Hagar reveals *El Roi* to Abraham, Sarah, and ultimately to us. Our God is "the God who sees me."

Hagar's story will preach to anyone who feels lost in someone else's story. Hagar is God's antidote to negative messages coming to us from others. For if a trafficked, forgotten, disposable slave girl matters to God and plays a vital part in God's purposes, none of our stories can safely be dismissed as minor.

> *O Lord, thank You that You are the God who sees me. Help me to draw strength from knowing I live under Your gaze and that I have a part to play today in what You are doing in this world.*

REFLECTION: Do you feel lost in someone else's story? What difference does it make for you *today* to know God sees you?

Journal, sketch, compose a poem, write a letter to God, meditate on a hymn or worship song that comes to mind.

Choosing to See

:: CHERI FULLER ::

*The land we passed through and explored
is exceedingly good. If the Lord is pleased with us, he
will lead us into that land, a land flowing with milk
and honey, and will give it to us.*

NUMBERS 14:7–8 NIV

One weekend I arrived at a beach, looking forward to walking in the white sand. What awaited me was the most putrid-smelling seaweed I'd ever encountered. Having been brought in by a storm and heated by the sun, the smelly blackish green seaweed was everywhere. No matter how far I walked, the first two days all I could see or smell was that awful seaweed. I barely noticed any of the beautiful things around me in the ocean or sky, and my mood became as disagreeable as the seaweed.

The next morning, however, when I went out, I noticed a blonde toddler splashing in the waves, and a father and his son making an intricate sand castle. They weren't letting the seaweed dictate their moods or ruin their day. Just then, the Lord turned my gaze up to the dazzling blue Texas sky and out to the sun gleaming off the water. The seaweed hadn't moved, but this time it didn't spoil my enjoyment because I was focusing on something else.

In this passage, Joshua and Caleb saw that the land God had sent them to explore was "exceedingly good"; they focused on the blessings God had in store there. The other men on the expedition saw only giants and obstacles and were filled with fear and spread a bad report. Ask the Lord to help you look up and keep your focus on Him—and not to miss the beautiful things along the way.

> *Lord Jesus, open my spiritual eyes to see the bless-*
> *ings and beauty in my path even in difficult times.*
> *Forgive me for focusing on the problems, the "stinky*
> *seaweed" in the world around me—and most of all,*
> *help me keep my eyes on You.*

REFLECTION: What is the "seaweed" in your own life that hinders your seeing the blessings in your path?

Journal, sketch, compose a poem, write a letter to God,
meditate on a hymn or worship song that comes to mind.

Anxiety

:: BEV HISLOP ::

He calls his own sheep by name and leads them out. . . .
He goes on ahead of them, and his sheep
follow him because they know his voice.

JOHN 10:3–4 NIV

I awoke with strong feelings of anxiety. They followed me into the car as I left for work. A filming of an online course segment was scheduled for ten o'clock and I did not feel fully prepared. As I was complaining to the Lord about this, I was suddenly distracted by the license plate on the car in front of mine. Typically I would never notice a license plate, even though the bumper-to-bumper traffic on this two-lane road might increase that possibility. In all the years I had traveled this familiar road to work, I had never noticed this car or this license plate. But there it was! I did a double take. *The license plate clearly had the year of my birth and my full initials!* I blinked in disbelief.

At that moment I sensed God saying to me, "Bev, I know all about you. I know you are feeling anxious this morning.

156

But in a similar way that this car is going before you, so am I today. Just follow Me closely, as you are this car. Remember Jesus' words? 'He calls his own sheep by name and leads them out . . . he goes on ahead of them, and his sheep follow him because they know his voice'" (John 10:3–4).

Oh Lord, forgive me for thinking this work task was all up to me, dependent totally on my abilities and full preparation . . .

The message was clear enough and the outcome of the day's filming confirmed the truth that our Good Shepherd still today "Calls his own sheep by name and leads them out." Like the car in front of me that day, Jesus also precedes you into wherever He leads you today.

> *Forgive me for not trusting You to lead me in a way that would more fully prepare my heart for today's assignments. Thank You for knowing me so well that You are fully prepared to provide all I need. What a Good Shepherd You are to me!*

REFLECTION: List your concerns. Picture the Good Shepherd walking in front of you carrying your burdens.

Journal, sketch, compose a poem, write a letter to God, meditate on a hymn or worship song that comes to mind.

Do You Want to Get Well?

:: HARMONY DUST ::

*When Jesus saw him lying there and learned that
he had been in this condition for a long time,
he asked him, "Do you want to get well?"*

JOHN 5:6 NIV

There is a well-told story of a man, lying on a mat, who had been disabled for thirty-eight years. In it, Jesus asks him a question: "Do you want to get well?" (John 5).

At that point, the man started coming up with excuses, saying that nobody would help him, and every time he tried to get better, somebody got in his way. Ultimately, Jesus instructs the man to "Get up! Pick up your mat and walk." He follows this instruction and is miraculously healed.

I believe that Jesus is asking you and me the same question: "Do you want to get well?"

Sometimes we think we want to get better, but when it comes down to it, we have a million excuses as to why we can't. We complain that nobody will help us and that every time we try, something gets in our way. We become comfortable with our condition and content to remain paralyzed on our mats.

I spent many years wishing my life would change, stuck in strip clubs, dysfunctional patterns, and unhealthy relationships. But ultimately, it wasn't enough to want to change—I had to decide to change.

Ultimately, the decision is in our hands. Nobody can want it for us. God won't force it on us. Our friends can't fix us. Finding the "right man" won't miraculously make our life better. We must decide to get well. Once we do, I believe that just as the paralytic man discovered, Jesus will give us the strength we need in order to walk.

> *Lord, lead me by ways I have not known. Help me begin to boldly step out of old conditions in my life. I ask You for healing and direction. Guide me along unfamiliar paths and make the rough places smooth. In Jesus' mighty name, Amen.*

REFLECTION: What "condition" (situation, habit, relationship) in your own life do you believe Jesus is asking you to step out of? What is preventing you from "getting well"?

Journal, sketch, compose a poem, write a letter to God, meditate on a hymn or worship song that comes to mind.

Tsunami of Grief

:: LAURA PETHERBRIDGE ::

*Without warning, a furious storm came up on the lake,
so that the waves swept over the boat.*

MATTHEW 8:24 NIV

April 7, 1984, went from being an innocent "normal" day to the worst day of my life. In an instant I discovered that my husband no longer wanted to be married. When I was eight years old, my parents decided to end their marriage. The pain and shame of that experience caused me to make a vow to myself—"I will never be divorced." My husband's devastating announcement shattered that dream and induced a steady flow of tears that didn't stop for a very long time.

During that season of loss and grief, I discovered a Jesus I never knew. His lavish compassion led me to trust the promises in His Word, rather than the villainous voices inside my head that whispered, "You're an ugly, pitiful failure—no one will ever love you." In the turbulent storm of divorce, Christ became my anchor.

In desperation I offered up my shattered heart. I asked Him to take the evil and disgrace intended to annihilate me, and use it for good.

My divorce scar now serves a higher calling. It points to the healing power of a faithful Savior who is willing to forgive, love, and comfort His beloved no matter the storm. People may abandon or disappoint us, but there is One who remains in the rocking boat holding us tightly, even when the ferocious waves of life threaten disaster.

Lord, I'm facing a storm that feels like a tsunami. I'm tired. And if I'm being honest, I'm beginning to question if You care or even exist. I'm embarrassed to admit that my faith, which was once strong, is now weak. I'm desperate, God. Today I'm making the decision to trust in You. Please show me how to keep my eyes on You when the waves seem exceedingly high, and the downpour is overflowing the boat. Help me to recognize the lies that threaten to crush my faith, and replace my fears with Your unshakeable confidence. Lord, remind me that nothing, absolutely nothing, can separate me from Your provision and Your unconditional love. Amen.

REFLECTION: Draw a picture or make a collage about the storm around you. How is God walking with you in it?

Journal, sketch, compose a poem, write a letter to God, meditate on a hymn or worship song that comes to mind.

In Control

:: JOANNE HEIM ::

God . . . the blessed controller of all things.
1 Timothy 6:15 Phillips

o you ever get tired of trying to control everything? In those occasional moments when you slow down and sit still, are you overwhelmed by feeling responsible for absolutely everything? Do you worry that if you stopped trying to control everything all the balls you juggle and all the plates you spin would come crashing down around you? You long to stop, you want to rest, but you keep on going out of habit because it's become second nature. At this point, you're not sure how *not* to control—or at least strive to control—everything.

And so you keep going as always—struggling to maintain control, grasping at ends, trying to make the pieces fit. But there's always something that won't be controlled, something that doesn't cooperate. You think you just might want to give up control, but wonder what would happen if you did.

I think many of us have a love/hate relationship with control. I know I certainly have! Striving to control things around us—ourselves, our jobs, our children, our circumstances—makes us feel important, worthwhile, necessary. Being in control makes us feel powerful. But working to control things around us also makes us feel exhausted, worn out, unhappy. Because no matter how hard we try, how many lists and schedules we make, the truth is that we cannot control everything.

It's not a matter of trying harder, of being more organized, of getting it together. We can't control everything because it's not what we were designed to do! Being in control is not our job. It is God's job.

"God . . . the blessed controller of all things." Not you. Not me. No wonder trying to control everything doesn't work well for us. We're trying to do a job we were not created or equipped to do. It's time to let go.

> *O God, I confess my desire to control all things. And my desire to give up control. Help me surrender today and to rest in Your blessed control of all things.*

REFLECTION: What are some things you've been wearing yourself out trying to control? Each time that desire to control those things surfaces today, deliberately hand it to God, praying, "You are the blessed controller of all things. This is not my job."

Journal, sketch, compose a poem, write a letter to God, meditate on a hymn or worship song that comes to mind.

The Holy Spirit's Nudge

:: ANITA LUSTREA ::

*I am telling you these things now while I am still with
you. But when the Father sends the Advocate
as my representative—that is, the Holy Spirit—
he will teach you everything and will remind
you of everything I have told you.*

JOHN 14:25–26 NLT

I met with a friend this morning. She's someone I don't
see all that often but have deep affection for. The Holy
Spirit had prompted me to call her just a couple of
days earlier to see if we could get together. I had a sense
something was wrong and that she might need to talk. I simply acted on a nudge from the Holy Spirit. Some call it a
prompting, I call it a nudge, author Bill Hybels calls it a God
whisper.

I remember years ago driving home after work, feeling an
overwhelming sense that I needed to turn down a certain
street to visit someone from church. I thought, "I don't have
time. What do I tell her when I knock at the door?" Regardless
of my excuses, the deep impression didn't go away. I turned

my car around, parked, and went to the door. My friend was tired and lonely. She was a new mom and really needed a word of encouragement. I not only got to be that encouraging word, but received the double blessing of seeing her spirits lifted and realizing I had listened and obeyed the nudge of the Holy Spirit of God.

My husband was preaching at church a few weeks ago and felt the prompting to give an altar call. What would have happened in the lives of the people who walked forward to do business with God if Mike hadn't heeded the Holy Spirit's nudge?

It's all about listening. I've never known the Holy Spirit to push or yell. I wonder how many times life has been too noisy or too busy for me to hear His voice?

The friend I met with was very glad I'd called. God used our time together to encourage and empower her. What if I hadn't picked up the phone?

Lord, help us listen to the nudges and whispers of
Your Holy Spirit, that we might make a difference for
You. Amen.

REFLECTION: Look for times this week when you can act on the Holy Spirit's nudge.

Journal, sketch, compose a poem, write a letter to God,
meditate on a hymn or worship song that comes to mind.

Come Out to Life

:: JANELLE HALLMAN ::

Jesus called in a loud voice, "Lazarus, come out!"
The dead man came out.

JOHN 11:43–44 NIV

*L*azarus's suffering, death, and "coming out" were prophetic. It gave us a preview of the Easter story. Lazarus's experience planted an image into the history of humankind that personifies the message that death is *not* the final word in God's kingdom. This image was to endure throughout the ages and bring hope to all of humankind.

Some might think that it was easy for Lazarus to "come out." After all, Jesus spoke to him directly. But what if Lazarus had been afraid? After all, he was surrounded by darkness, stench, and grave clothes. What if he believed that the agony of being awakened in death was actually worse than the previous agony of suffering and slowly dying? What if he struggled with shame? Indeed, as a dead man, his culture considered him unclean—utterly untouchable. Perhaps he somehow felt relieved by death. When you are dead, no one can hurt you—what is there left to hurt? In darkness, no one can see the pain, the confusion, the shame, or the guilt.

I have worked with many women who have felt as if they were dead or at least living in darkness as they walked deeper and deeper into lesbianism. For some, it starts with an extremely close friendship that turns emotionally dependent and eventually sexual. Often these women are misunderstood and judged harshly by their church communities. To survive, many hide from everyone and everything, inadvertently entombing their very souls.

Some of these women have heard Jesus speak loudly, "Come out!" The truth is, though, for most it is extremely difficult to "come out." After all, people usually don't come back to life nor do many women choose to come out of lesbianism. When God asks a woman to step into the light, she must face her humanity, her pain, her brokenness, and her sin and shame. Each time the light hits an area that was previously dead, it may hurt. But in the light, there is also hope for healing, freedom, and love. Every step any of us make toward the light indeed testifies to the power of the resurrection.

Dear Lord, please breathe new life into those inner parts that seem dead, listless, or without hope.

REFLECTION: What is the risk of letting go of the old and taking hold of a new life?

Journal, sketch, compose a poem, write a letter to God, meditate on a hymn or worship song that comes to mind.

Family History

:: BEV HUBBLE TAUKE ::

*But if they will confess their sins and
the sins of their fathers . . . I will remember
the covenant with their ancestors.*

LEVITICUS 26:40,45 NIV

I spent years resenting my husband, who refused to discipline our sons—dumping hard parenting on me," reported a woman at one of my family workshops. "One day I asked him, 'So how did your father discipline you?'"

"'He'd line us up against the wall,' said my husband, 'then pull out his gun. Waving it our way, he said the next one who disobeys—this is what you get!'"

"At that moment," said the woman, "I saw my husband as a walking wound—deserving more compassion from me."

This husband sent a surge of healing through his family when he confessed old family failures. The Leviticus promise doesn't always work this dramatically—but researchers report powerful evidence that those who take inventory of family history often boost emotional and relationship healing.

I've seen this principle activated in many ways. Years ago, my cousin and I visited a favorite family elder, asking him to describe his own youth. Among many anecdotes from the early 1900s, he told how one young sibling literally took the clothes off her sister's back when she wore clothing her sister had already chosen for school.

"So that explains it," we exclaimed to each other after our encounter.

This pampered relative had for decades been a major family *wounder*—but seemed oblivious. Well, no wonder. As author C. S. Lewis has noted, mindless indulgence is no act of love. Programmed by parents and siblings to feel entitled from an early age, she was denied opportunities to develop character, social radar, or empathy, producing a nature experienced by others as radioactive.

Our family elder's spontaneous confession of old dysfunctions clarified family history and recalibrated hearts and minds down the line. My cousin and I found ourselves empowered emotionally and spiritually through greater understanding and compassion for wounded and *wounder* relatives, alike.

> *Dear Heavenly Father, please help me own my family history, so I can realign my mind and heart with truth, and invite Your blessing.*

REFLECTION: Will you begin to embrace your own family pain? Jesus walks with you in your tears.

Journal, sketch, compose a poem, write a letter to God, meditate on a hymn or worship song that comes to mind.

Global Sisters

:: LYNNE HYBELS ::

*For he will deliver the needy who cry out, the afflicted
who have no one to help . . . He will rescue them
from oppression and violence,
for precious is their blood in his sight.*

PSALM 72:12, 14 NIV

As I have traveled internationally, I have been shocked to discover how many of the world's injustices disproportionately impact women and girls. Overall, women and girls are the least valued, least fed, least educated, and least protected people group in the world.

Recently I visited the Democratic Republic of the Congo—arguably the worse place on earth to be a woman. In a horrible civil war raging for over a decade, one weapon used by soldiers on all sides of the conflict is rape. So thousands of women and little girls have been brutally violated. It was heartbreaking to talk with women who have been so violently abused, and I came home committed to raising awareness and funds to help them.

Something good happens in me whenever I engage with my global sisters. When I visit them, talk with them, pray for them, or raise money for them, I am enriched. I feel like I've just moved closer to the heart of God—and the truth is, I have. Because every woman on the face of this earth means as much to God as I do, or my mother and daughter and friends do, or you do. God wants to deliver each one of them; and ours are the hands and hearts He wants to use to do it.

Imagine what a difference American women could make if we each addressed just one of the needs faced by our global sisters! We could raise money for a refugee mom. Sponsor an AIDS orphan. Buy products made by women rescued from sex trafficking. One quick Google search can yield hundreds of opportunities.

None of us can respond to all the needs in the world, but we cannot afford to be overwhelmed and paralyzed. We each can—and must—do something.

God, what is mine to do? Give me the willingness to ask that question earnestly and the courage to respond in a tangible way.

REFLECTION: What tragedy or injustice that impacts women brings tears to your eyes whenever you hear about it? What's one step you can take in response—today?

Journal, sketch, compose a poem, write a letter to God, meditate on a hymn or worship song that comes to mind.

Growing Up

:: MELINDA SCHMIDT ::

Let the children come to me.
Don't stop them! For the Kingdom of God
belongs to those who are like these children.

LUKE 18:16 NLT

*Y*ou're like a little girl in the sandbox, waiting for someone to come by and rescue you.

A friend was challenging me to examine the way I was habitually processing some childhood wounds. I had to admit it—I was stuck in the sandbox. That word picture spoke powerfully to me, and the tug in my heart confirmed my friend wasn't wrong.

We bring all of who we are to our present adult life. The whole of our life experience. In my growing up, I had tried to keep the first ten years of my life (ones I remembered as a skinny, cat's eye–glasses wearing, humiliatingly short-banged, insecure, and alone little girl) tucked in a basket on the front of my bike as I pedaled into adulthood. But that little girl was beginning to fight her way back into my life, pushing the lid off of that basket, letting me know she was there.

I wrote in my journal,

To run through yards in dirty socks . . . pebbles and bits of twig . . . in pink sneakers with white laces . . . the smell of outdoors in my hair . . . to laugh and live . . . what is imagined— . . . that's living at its best.

And,

Heaven will be living . . . that grinning child . . . shining back at me . . . from the puddle.

Bringing the whole of me—all of me, every year of me—to my present life means spending time with that little girl who wants to be known, even though I have tried to hide her away.

What does she have to tell me? What is she afraid of? What does she long for? Who is she really?

> *Jesus, You desire the whole of us, not the part we choose to bring. Help us to courageously recognize and process the years of us that we want to dismiss. We know that You go with us.*

REFLECTION: What photo, your own sketch, or other symbol expresses who you are? Has it changed over time? What does this picture tell you about the deepest places of your soul?

Journal, sketch, compose a poem, write a letter to God, meditate on a hymn or worship song that comes to mind.

Speaking Truth

:: DEE BRESTIN ::

*Rather, speaking the truth in love, we are to grow up
in every way into him who is the head, into Christ.*

EPHESIANS 4:15 ESV

"A my" wrote to my website: *"Pamela" is always late.
Last week I held our booth at Panera for twenty
minutes. She breezed in saying, "Sorry! Every light
I hit was red!" I was quiet, but festering, feeling she didn't care
about me. Yet I don't want to lose a friendship over this. Should
I just live with it?*

How do we live out Ephesians 4:15 in friendship? Get
alone with the Lord and be still, asking Him to show you anything in your heart. So often I hear from women who are
angry with a friend who doesn't give them as much time as
they want—often they have idolized that friend, putting her in
the place of God.

If He shows you your friend has a sin that should be addressed, then prepare to speak the truth in love:

- Pray for wisdom and favor.
- Begin each sentence with "I" instead of "You," so it isn't accusatory.
- Make sure *every* sentence, not just the opening and closing, are filled with love. (Forget the sandwich approach: A compliment, a hard thing, then sandwiched by a compliment. Everyone has trouble eating that sandwich.)
- Tell her what you would like to see happen.

E-mail and Facebook are terrible ways to confront. The best way is face-to-face so you can be sensitive to her face and hear her. Amy might say: "I care a lot about our friendship. I feel hurt each time I wait for you, feeling like I am not valued. I know that is not your intent—but is there a way you can help me?"

If Pamela agrees to try to be more punctual but doesn't change, then Amy will need to decide if she can live with it. Often, we can live with weaknesses by remembering God's grace to us.

> *Lord, search my heart and root out sin in me. If You do lead me to confront someone, please prepare my words, filling them with love, and prepare her heart.*

REFLECTION: In the above, put yourself in Pamela's place. How would you best want to be confronted?

Journal, sketch, compose a poem, write a letter to God, meditate on a hymn or worship song that comes to mind.

Hope in the Midst of Infertility

:: MARLO SCHALESKY ::

Put your hope in God.
PSALM 43:5 NIV

I always hoped for a godly husband, three children, a dog, and a white picket fence. I hoped for good health, a great job, and success in my field. I hoped for the "happily ever after" part of the fairy tale, and wanted nothing to do with the parts filled with dragons and despair.

But God had other plans.

It wasn't until I faced infertility and the loss of all my dreams that I really began to understand what it meant to put my hope in God, in God alone.

Failed medical treatments taught me I couldn't put my hope in medicine. Doctors were no guarantee of success. Surgeries and painful shots taught me not to put my hope in health. Expensive procedures taught me that I couldn't put my hope in my bank account. Failure itself taught me that I couldn't put my hope in myself or in my own ability to make my dreams come true. I couldn't put hope in circumstance;

I couldn't trust in luck. And I certainly couldn't put my hope in children that I might never have.

Only God was left.

So I discovered that He alone has the power to run my life. He is the only place I can put my hope and not be disappointed. I can't put my hope in anything except the belief that God is ordering my life well, in knowing that He loves me. I can put my hope in His promises of eternal life and assurance that He is with me always. I can put my hope in God alone. Everything else will fail.

> *Lord, I want to put my hope in You alone. Please show me those places in my life where I've placed my hope in things other than You. Help me to loosen my fingers and let go of my own hopes and dreams so that I might embrace Yours. Show me the wonder of knowing You, and help me to trust Your amazing love for me no matter what my circumstances hold.*

REFLECTION: Focus on the prayer above with open hands in front of you, symbolizing letting go of what's cluttering your heart.

Journal, sketch, compose a poem, write a letter to God, meditate on a hymn or worship song that comes to mind.

How to Really Love

:: JULIANNA SLATTERY ::

*Therefore, as God's chosen people, holy and dearly
loved, clothe yourselves with compassion, kindness,
humility, gentleness and patience. Bear with each
other and forgive whatever grievances you may have
against one another. Forgive as the Lord forgave you.
And over all these virtues put on love, which binds
them all together in perfect unity.*

COLOSSIANS 3:12–14 NIV

few years ago, I read these verses and started
praying, *Lord, help me to treat other people like
this . . . to be compassionate, kind, gentle, forgiving, and loving.* I really thought the Lord would convict me to
make cookies for my neighbor. Instead, the conviction from
the Holy Spirit came from a whole different angle. *Juli, love
your husband.* Overall, I am pretty loving toward my husband.
However, I don't always love him in the way he would like to
receive love, specifically, physical intimacy. Honestly, there
are times that I would rather love him in every other way. I'm
willing to make his favorite dinner and listen patiently about

struggles at work, but in this one area, I am naturally selfish, unforgiving, and insensitive.

I've learned over the years that many other wives have similar struggles. A woman may be willing to sell all of her earthly goods and move to Africa to serve the Lord, but she can't quite muster the strength to love her husband sexually. The sexual relationship, in many marriages, is the most tangible and difficult way to show love. I've rarely met a couple who hasn't encountered some conflict in the bedroom. Any number of serious roadblocks (issues from the past, physical ailments, differing levels of desire, body image issues, and pornography, to name a few) keep them from enjoying the gift of sexual intimacy.

Perhaps the Lord has allowed these roadblocks in sexual intimacy for a purpose: to teach us how to really love. If we only give or forgive when we feel like doing so, we are not really loving. God defines love as self-denial, sacrifice, and forgiveness. It is only when we encounter differences or conflict that we can truly be clothed in love.

> *Lord, teach me to look at everything, including marital intimacy, through Your eyes. Help me to be clothed with compassion, kindness, gentleness, patience, forgiveness, and love toward my husband.*

REFLECTION: What would it look like for you to be clothed with Paul's teaching in Colossians 3:12–14 as you address difficulties in marital intimacy?

Journal, sketch, compose a poem, write a letter to God, meditate on a hymn or worship song that comes to mind.

God's Great Love

:: HELEN CEPERO ::

How great is the love the Father has lavished on us,
that we should be called children of God!
And that is what we are!

1 JOHN 3:1 NIV

The percussionist in the back of the beginners' band is only rarely hitting the snare drum on the beat. But nobody could miss in his wide, toothy smile the pure joy he finds in hearing those drumsticks make that reverberating racket. The frustrated band director audibly hums the theme to himself while directing each and every beat, but neither the band nor the audience is paying any attention to him.

Next to me, a mother's eyes are brimming as she watches just one band member. "That's my son Darrin in the back, playing the snare drum. Isn't he just great?" Whispering back to her, my eyes fill with tears as well, as I point out to her the trumpeter who sits in the fourth chair of the second row, "And that's my daughter Leah—just look at her."

She nods, smiles, hands me a tissue and we both wipe our eyes, eagerly awaiting the next raucous number.

I admit it. I have always loved beginners' band concerts. It might be easy to miss the concentration of awkward effort, the willingness to try something new, and the courage to try it together with others. But we mothers do not miss the music that is both within our own child and beyond them as well.

Many of us have the idea as we live out a life of faith that God plays the role of the band director frustrated at our inability to make proper music or even find the beat. But what if God is really more like the mothers who watch their own with rapt attention? What if, when God looks at each of us and sees our longing to live in Him, tears well up in those holy eyes? What if He sees in our willingness to play the music of our faith the possibility of living into another way of being?

God, You call us Your daughters and sons. May our music together and alone be motivated not by fear but by Your great love.

REFLECTION: How has my understanding of God helped or hindered me in playing my own faith's music?

Journal, sketch, compose a poem, write a letter to God, meditate on a hymn or worship song that comes to mind.

You Are Recognized

:: JULIE-ALLYSON IERON ::

Lord, You have searched me and known me. . . .
Before a word is on my tongue, You know all
about it, Lord. You have encircled me;
You have placed Your hand on me.

PSALM 139:1, 4–5 HCSB

A friend I hadn't seen since grad school found me online and commented about my, shall we say, new and improved hair color. Then she said, "But I'd still recognize your face anywhere."

This got me thinking about how our Master recognizes us. He knows our words before we speak them; our thoughts before we think them; our actions before we take them. Jesus said our Father numbers the hairs on our heads (Matthew 10:30)—a sign of His loving care for even the minutiae of our lives. (I guess He recognizes the hairs, no matter what color I paint them.)

In response to this knowledge, we can be comforted or paralyzed. Paralyzed in fear because we're laid bare, shown up as soiled in light of the Almighty's purity. Yet comforted because, if we're in Christ, only His gracious, redeeming love will touch us.

I choose to take comfort in God's knowledge of me. This is a crucial choice for me, as a caregiver for my parents and a speaker whose ministry encourages, equips, and strengthens caregivers when their daily lives overflow with exhausting minutiae. Caregivers, especially, need the comfort of knowing that the Master of the Universe takes note of every detail of life. And knowing it all, He encircles us with His mighty hand.

The word picture David used for *encircling* describes someone attaching a money bag to his wrist. Someone values the money and takes precautions to secure it for transport. Similarly, Someone values us and takes precautions to secure us for transport to our eternal home.

Caregiver or not, anyone tempted to feel alone, forgotten, or unrecognizable behind the colors of change life brings can bask in this knowledge.

> *God, I'm grateful that You attach me like a valuable money bag to Your hand—that You care for me even though You know absolutely everything about me. Let me be peacefully aware of Your nearness all day. Amen.*

REFLECTION: Where do you see reminders of God's care for you? What evidence do you see of how much God values you? How does that influence the way you value yourself?

Journal, sketch, compose a poem, write a letter to God, meditate on a hymn or worship song that comes to mind.

Extravagant Love

:: SHANNON ETHRIDGE ::

*"When that day comes," says the Lord, "you will call
me 'my husband' instead of 'my master.' I will make
you my wife forever, showing you righteousness
and justice, unfailing love and compassion.
I will be faithful to you and make you mine,
and you will finally know me as the Lord."*

HOSEA 2:16, 19–20 NLT

*D*uring the first months of dating, I hesitated to give Greg
Ethridge my whole heart. Why? Because he was such a
good guy. Greg had never rebelled against God or his
parents. He had never fallen away from church. He had never
engaged in premarital sex. I, however, had done all those
things, and was dragging around a boatload of guilt and
shame as a result.

One night I offered Greg a free jump-ship pass. "A good
guy like you deserves better than a girl like me," I explained.

Imagine my relief when he responded, "Shannon, your
past makes absolutely no difference. I love you for who you

are today and for who God made you to be, and I want to help you become that woman."

One of the biggest hindrances that keeps us from enjoying a more intimate relationship with our heavenly Bridegroom is the same feeling —that such a good God couldn't possibly love such a not-so-good person. But God passionately woos and pursues us, determined to win our affections in spite of our flaws.

He promises to be faithful to you, even when you are unfaithful to Him. His love for you is not conditional. He will never turn His back on you, wouldn't dream of slamming the door and driving away, or ripping your heart out and stomping on it. God is different from any lover you have ever had or anyone who has ever given up on you. Most people have their limits as to how much they can take in a relationship. Not God. He loves you without limits, and He wants you to love Him without limits as well.

> *Creator God, thank You for looking beyond our weaknesses and pursuing us with Your extravagant love. Give us hearts to love You extravagantly in return!*

REFLECTION: Do I question the level of commitment that my heavenly Bridegroom has for me? What is getting in the way of believing He loves me deeply?

Journal, sketch, compose a poem, write a letter to God, meditate on a hymn or worship song that comes to mind.

What to Do?

:: CAROL KENT ::

In my desperation I prayed, and the Lord listened;
he saved me from all my troubles.

PSALM 34:6 NLT

Ten years ago my husband and I received a middle-of-the-night phone call that forever changed our lives.

Our only child, a graduate of the U.S. Naval Academy, had been arrested for the murder of his wife's first husband. As nausea swept over me, I felt sick and numb simultaneously. In my darkest hour I wailed, "God, help us! Please protect my son from being attacked by other inmates. Help us to find an attorney quickly. Comfort the family of the deceased. I don't know what to do!"

Over the next few days, I wasn't sure God was listening. As I struggled to keep functioning in the middle of a heartache that was too big to manage, I slowly began to see a pattern. God's way of meeting our needs was through the compassionate help of fellow Christians. Some sent cards. Meals were left on our doorstep. Yellow roses came from two of my sisters with a note saying: "You once gave us some decorating advice. You told us that yellow flowers will brighten any room. We thought you needed a little yellow in your life right now." Friends dropped by to hug us and assure us of their prayers. Others sent checks. Some just came and wept with us.

We went through seven postponements of the trial over a period of two and a half years. Eventually, our twenty-five-year-old son was convicted and sentenced to life in prison without the possibility of parole. As the news media flashed cameras in our faces, we walked away from the courthouse, held each other, and sobbed. The agony was palpable. The next day an overnight package arrived from one of our praying friends. It was filled with Kleenex and a note of encouragement. Sometimes God rescues us from our troubles with the hands and feet of His ambassadors who cover us with support and prayer.

Father, in the middle of my daily challenges, I will pray first and then look for Your deliverance. Help me not to miss Your answer in the form of people who touch my life with Christlike compassion. Amen.

REFLECTION: In what surprising way has God comforted you this week?

Journal, sketch, compose a poem, write a letter to God, meditate on a hymn or worship song that comes to mind.

Stir It Up

:: DANNA DEMETRE ::

*And if the Spirit of him who raised Jesus from the dead
is living in you, he who raised Christ from the dead
will also give life to your mortal bodies
through his Spirit, who lives in you.*

ROMANS 8:11 NIV

My sixteen-year struggle with bulimia helps me understand women who feel like they are in bondage to food. I know what it's like to be out of control—believing that change is impossible. I also know that "with God all things are possible." Thirty years ago, I didn't simply lose weight and keep it off—I found lasting victory over all my "food issues."

After years of coaching women toward healthier lifestyles, I've realized the most important truth women need to embrace is the power of the Holy Spirit to renew and transform the mind. As the verse above tells us, the very same Spirit that raised Jesus from the dead is alive and living in us and can infuse us with power to deal with all life's challenges —even our habits!

Sadly, in our greatest weakness, we often fail to walk in the Spirit, but instead walk in the weakness of our flesh. God has done His part, but we must do ours. I hope this simple illustration helps you, as it did me: Imagine that you are a glass of milk and the Holy Spirit is chocolate syrup. When you're saved, God infuses you with His Spirit—plop—the "syrup" drops to the bottom of the glass, but the Spirit has not yet mixed fully, so the milk is still white. To "activate" the Spirit in your life, you stir it up through faith, Scripture, prayer, and worship. When we intentionally use God's Word in our areas of struggle, it helps us cut out the lies we believe and replace them with life-changing truth. So, grab your spoon—the Bible, faith, prayer, and worship—and stir. "Chocolate" never tasted so good!

> *Heavenly Father, thank You for Your Word and for the gift of Your Holy Spirit living in me. Please help me to activate Your power through faith, prayer, worship, and Scripture.*

REFLECTION: Offer up your weakness to Jesus today. In faith, walk in His Spirit even if your steps feel timid.

Journal, sketch, compose a poem, write a letter to God, meditate on a hymn or worship song that comes to mind.

Dark Soul

:: JILL RIGBY GARNER ::

*I sought the Lord, and he answered me; he delivered
me from all my fears. Those who look to him are
radiant; their faces are never covered with shame.*

PSALM 34:4–5 NIV

I worried about my husband. Nothing could satisfy his
soul. I prayed his discontentment would turn back to
pleasure, but my dreaded fear came true. He left our
home to live on the other side of town.

Darkness filled my soul. Looking in the mirror I saw the
face of someone I no longer knew. The woman looking back at
me wasn't me, but a lost soul abandoned and unloved. The
more I looked in the mirror for answers, the fewer I found.
Each glance in the mirror served as a reminder of who I once
was, but no longer could be. The days of summer passed with
little hope. Soon, falling leaves created a blanket of color
across the landscape.

One chilly morning, I wandered from my lonely bedroom
to the kitchen. The sound of my breathing pierced the hushed

still as I stood before an expanse of windows gazing at the world. The early morning sun filtered through barren trees and warmed my cold body. As the sunlight poured through the window, the love of God penetrated my heart, igniting new passion. Light from the presence of the Son brought truth, removing shame and restoring confidence. Warmth from the great Counselor filled my soul with fresh purpose. The eyes of my heart opened to the possibilities of a new life filled with more love than I had ever known. Looking in the mirror had shown me the woman I once was; looking through the window revealed the woman I could become.

Each of us shares the same need, to be known and loved. The world holds a mirror before us telling us to love ourselves. God calls us to the window to say, "Love Me. I've always loved you."

> *Sweet Father, open the eyes of my heart to see You as never before. To accept Your great love for one such as I . . . afraid, lonely, lost, searching. Keep me from looking any further for the love I so desperately seek. May I rest and grow in Your love. Through Jesus, Amen.*

REFLECTION: Will you live your life in the mirror or at the window?

Journal, sketch, compose a poem, write a letter to God, meditate on a hymn or worship song that comes to mind.

Healing from Shame

:: BECKY HARLING ::

Those who look to him are radiant;
their faces are never covered with shame.

PSALM 34:5 NIV

The woman who looks to God is promised a radiant face. So, if your face isn't radiant, why not? Chances are it's not because you're using the wrong facial cream. It might be because shame is dragging your face down. Girl-friend, what you need is a facelift!

How can you tell if shame is making your face droop? The woman held captive by shame believes the lie that she is worthless, bad, and inferior. Those messages may come from her childhood. Shame is often the result of abuse or neglect. Or, she may have internalized shame because though she has confessed past sin, she still feels guilty. Either way, if your face is covered with shame, you are listening to the voice of the accuser. The good news is that God wants to give you a spiritual facelift (see Psalm 3:3).

Healing from shame begins when you look up into the

face of Jesus. He calls you holy, precious, and dearly loved (see Colossians 3:12). He died, taking your shame, so that you would no longer be held captive. He whispers, "I love you. By my wounds you are healed" (see Isaiah 53:5). That's God's part in your healing. Here's your part: Identify and replace the lies you have believed with the truth found in God's Word. Every time Satan starts with his "blah, blah, blah," accusing you and trying to cover your face in shame, clobber him with Scripture! Then choose to praise God for His love. When you praise Him, your thoughts are focused on Him instead of the messages of your past, and the Holy Spirit quickens your heart toward deeper faith. Before you know it, your face will be glowing with a radiance that comes only from God.

> *Lord Jesus, how I praise You that those who look to You are offered healing from shame. Show me how to replace the lies from my childhood with the truth found in Your Word. Rather than being held captive by shame, help me today to fix my eyes on You so that my face will reflect Your radiance.*

REFLECTION: What messages have you received that left you with feelings of shame?

Journal, sketch, compose a poem, write a letter to God, meditate on a hymn or worship song that comes to mind.

Mourning to Dancing

:: JANET THOMPSON ::

God will let you laugh again;
you'll raise the roof with shouts of joy.

JOB 8:21 THE MESSAGE

W hen I was diagnosed with breast cancer and had a recurrence six years later, I had to search to find something to be joyful about. In the midst of the initial fear, pain, and sadness, there was little happiness or laughter. No one with breast cancer, or any disease, is ecstatic or delighted with the diagnosis. If we could choose, most would say *please pass me by* with this character-building experience. But our illness did not catch God by surprise. Solomon, the wisest man who ever lived besides Jesus, said, "When times are good, be happy; but when times are bad, consider this: God has made the one as well as the other" (Ecclesiastes 7:14 NIV).

Often we have to act our way into a feeling, and sometimes that's what it takes to pull ourselves out of a down mood. Happiness and joy really are our choice, and they usually accompany gratitude. The day before my first surgery, I held my five-week-old grandson in my arms, and I was smiling with happiness and joy for this precious new life in our family. Six years later after my second surgery, that same grandson and his two brothers and sister made me a beautiful pink blanket covered in ribbons, hearts, and hand-braided fringe, and I was grinning ear to ear snuggled warm and secure under this gift of love. I had much to be happy about.

Spend time quietly reading a few passages from your Bible—God will meet you there. He'll remind you that no matter what the outcome of this latest trial, He will restore that sometimes-elusive happiness, and you will laugh and raise the roof with joy again.

> *Father, You know my painful circumstances and the sorrow I am experiencing. Please turn my mourning into dancing again. Put a smile on my face that shows the world my happiness doesn't depend on the things of this world; my joy is found in the promise that Your plans for me are good. Amen.*

REFLECTION: How do you picture happiness and joy in the future? Can that vision help you to live in your present circumstance? Offer that picture as a prayer to God.

Journal, sketch, compose a poem, write a letter to God, meditate on a hymn or worship song that comes to mind.

Global Compassion

:: SHAYNE MOORE ::

If you spend yourselves in behalf of the hungry and satisfy the needs of the oppressed, then your light will rise in the darkness, and your night will become like the noonday. The Lord will guide you always.

ISAIAH 58:10–12 NIV

Scripture is very consistent with the idea that caring for the needs of others is a serious issue when it comes to our spiritual formation and well-being. Women are the caretakers of the world. For most of us, caring for the world means caring for our immediate family and their needs. How, as busy women and moms, can we care for our own and at the same time develop as global thinkers tuned in to the needs of families worldwide?

All human beings are made in the image of God, and God intends for us to reflect Him to our world, to our generation. It is a beautiful mystery that God has enlisted us to act on His behalf in the project of healing creation. Jesus brought the reality of a healed world through His resurrection. We have the power of Christ's resurrection to act on behalf of justice and

196

compassion and reflect God to a suffering world.

As a Christian woman who lives in comfortable North America, what is my role? What can I really do to make a difference on a global level? I have come to believe spending ourselves on behalf of the poor and oppressed starts in our own kitchens, in our own homes. As Christian women we can educate ourselves about issues of extreme poverty and the HIV/AIDS pandemic.

We can educate others, take action by calling our leaders, and raise our voices in our churches about the things that break our hearts.

Jesus, as we engage issues of global need, give us thick skin and tender hearts.

REFLECTION: Do you feel your life is too full to engage issues of global need in a meaningful way? If so, what or who do you feel is limiting your involvement?

Journal, sketch, compose a poem, write a letter to God, meditate on a hymn or worship song that comes to mind.

Honoring Dreams

:: MELINDA SCHMIDT ::

*Who would have said to Abraham that
Sarah would nurse a baby? Yet I have given
Abraham a son in his old age!*

GENESIS 21:7 NLT

*O*ur dreams? Dreams are our hopes with wings! Whether
or not they find a spot to land and come to life, well,
that's a big question in life, isn't it. Do I deserve my
dreams? Will they come true?

Scottish singer Susan Boyle came to international attention when she appeared as a contestant on reality TV show
Britain's Got Talent in 2009. She told the judges her dream was
to be a professional singer, as successful as actress and
recording artist Elaine Page. The crowd jeered at that, but
eventually became her friend and rose to its feet as she began
to sing. After taking second place in the competition, she
released her first album in 2009 and acquired three Guinness
World Records based on its success.

Recently, as my husband, Dave, and I considered some

new opportunities, my friend, author Donna VanLiere, e-mailed me, "The plans of the Lord stand firm forever. He isn't thinking, 'They're thinking about doing *what*? Shocking. I didn't see that coming!' He plants desires and seeds and then waits for us to ask, seek, and knock!!" In their book *Women of the Bible*, authors Ann Spangler and Jean Syswerda write, "God hints at his purpose for you by planting dreams within your heart."

> *Lord, help me to honor my dreams and sort them out wisely. I need Your wisdom to know which ones I should purposefully pursue. I want to actively en-gage with You as I consider the dreams in my heart.*

REFLECTION: Take several passes at this: write out your dreams. If you could do anything, be anything, what or who would you be? How long have you held your dreams in your heart? Are there tears you need to shed, anger you need to process over dormant dreams? If you feel comfortable, begin to share your dream with wise others. Commit to praying the prayer above, or one that you write yourself.

Journal, sketch, compose a poem, write a letter to God, meditate on a hymn or worship song that comes to mind.

Acknowledgments

We appreciate all of the contributors to *Tending the Soul* whose unique messages we've been privileged to feature daily on *Midday Connection*. Our listeners continue to support and challenge us through their regular feedback. We're grateful to this growing community of women who have become such an important part of our lives.

We want to thank some men in our lives who have supported the vision, mission, and values of *Midday Connection*:

- Our husbands, Mike Murphy, David Schmidt, and John Neff
- Our coworkers at Moody Radio, *Midday Connection* Engineer Josh Klos, as well as Tim Svoboda, Chris Segard, and Joe Carlson

:: ABOUT THE CONTRIBUTORS ::

KRISTEN ANDERSON is an author, speaker, and founder of Reaching You Ministries. In her book *Life, In Spite of Me*, she shares the miracle of her survival of a suicide attempt and the hope that has completely transformed her life, giving her a powerful purpose for living. For more information about Kristen, please visit her website: http://reachingyouministries.com.

SHELLY BEACH is founder and director of the Cedar Falls Christian Writers' Workshop in Iowa and cofounder of the Breathe Christian Writers' Workshop in Michigan. Shelly is a graduate of Oakland University (BA) and Grand Rapids Theological Seminary (MRE). She and her husband, Dan, reside in Rockford, Michigan. Visit www.shellybeachonline.com.

TRISH BERG is author of *Rattled—Surviving Your Baby's First Year without Losing Your Cool; The Great American Supper Swap—Solving the Busy Woman's Family Dinnertime Dilemma;* and *A Scrapbook of Christmas Firsts—Stories to Warm Your Heart and Tips to Simplify Your Holiday.* A nationally recognized speaker, she has been a featured guest on television and radio, and her articles have appeared in numerous publications. You can connect with Trish on Facebook, Twitter, and at www.TrishBerg.com.

TRACEY BIANCHI coordinates women's ministry and is also a member of the worship teaching team at Christ Church of Oak Brook, a congregation of over two thousand located just outside of Chicago. Tracey is a freelance writer and speaker for a variety of national and international organizations. She is the author of *Green Mama: The Guilt Free Guide to Helping You and Your Kids Save the Planet.* Most important, she's the mama of three fabulous children and is married to an amazing man named Joel. Visit www.traceybianchi.com.

DEE BRESTIN has had a profound impact on the hearts of women through her internationally published Bible studies. Dee's first book was *The Friendships of Women*, a million-copy bestseller. She paired with Kathy Troccoli to write the trilogy *Falling in Love with Jesus. The God of All Comfort—Finding Your Way into His Arms* sprang from her own grief journey after losing her husband, Steve, to colon cancer. Dee is a frequent guest on *Focus on the Family* and *Midday Connection*. Go to www.deebrestin.com.

NICOLE BRADDOCK BROMLEY is the founder and director of OneVOICE enterprises and an international spokesperson on issues related to sexual abuse and human trafficking. She is the author of *Hush: Moving from Silence to Healing after Childhood Sexual Abuse* and *Breathe: Finding Freedom to Thrive in Relationships after Childhood Sexual Abuse*. She is a frequently featured guest on television and radio broadcasts around the world. Nicole and her husband, Matthew, have two sons. See www.onevoiceenterprises.com.

MINDY CALIGUIRE is the founder of Soul Care, a spiritual formation ministry, and director of transformation ministry for the Willow Creek Association. She is a contributing editor for *Conversations Journal*, and also serves as a frequent speaker and leadership consultant. Her books include *Discovering Soul Care, Spiritual Friendship, Soul Searching,* and *Simplicity*, as well as *Write for Your Soul: The Whys and Hows of Journaling*, with her husband, Jeff. Mindy, Jeff, and their three adventurous teenagers are all active members at Willow Creek Community Church. Visit www.soulcare.com.

HELEN CEPERO is a spiritual director, retreat leader, and teacher living in Anchorage, Alaska. She is the author of *Journaling as a Spiritual Practice: Encountering God through Attentive Writing* as well as of other journal articles and essays. Currently, Helen is an online instructor for North Park Theological Seminary, Chicago, and for Multnomah Biblical Seminary in Portland, as well as an adjunct instructor in Anchorage. She and her husband, Max Lopez-Cepero, have three adult children. Visit http://helencepero.net.

ROBIN CHADDOCK is an insightful speaker, seminar leader, internationally known author, and life coach. She teaches community college with a focus on life skills and career discernment. Robin earned a BA in psychology from Indiana's Taylor University, her MA in theology from California's Fuller Theological Seminary, and a DMin from Illinois' McCormick Theological Seminary. She and her husband, David, and their two children live in Indiana. Her weekly e-mail "Soul Snacks for Zesty Living" brings humor, encouragement, and insight to her readers. See www.RobinChaddock.com.

JANET DAVIS uses her years of work as a hospital chaplain, speaker, and spiritual director to glean wisdom and insight as she has listened to her own life and those of others. Her first book is *The Feminine Soul: Surprising Ways the Bible Speaks to Women*. The personal story featured in her devotion here is adapted from her new book, *Sacred Healing: MRIs, Marigolds, and Miracles*. Janet and her husband, Bob, live in Austin, Texas, where she enjoys gardening, good food, and any time spent with their four adult children. Go to www.janetdavisonline.com.

DR. ROSALIE DE ROSSET is a professor at the Moody Bible Institute, writer, literary/ social commentator, and conference speaker.

JENNIFER DEGLER, PhD, is a licensed psychologist, life coach, and co-author of *No More Christian Nice Girl: When Just Being Nice—Instead of Good—Hurts You, Your Family, and Your Friends*. A frequent speaker at women's events and marriage retreats, she also maintains a counseling practice, seeing adults, children, and couples for psychotherapy. She has been interviewed by numerous media outlets. Jennifer and her husband, Jeff, live in Lexington, Kentucky, with their two teenage children. Visit www.jenniferdegler.com.

DANNA DEMETRE has a diverse professional background—a registered nurse specializing in labor and delivery, corporate marketing manager for a Fortune 100 company, fitness professional, lifestyle coach, and a Christian talk radio host. A popular retreat and conference speaker, Danna is also the author of the bestselling: *Scale Down* and other books. Danna and her husband, Lew, have three adult children and live in San Diego with their fourteen-year-old adopted grandson, Jesse—a late life gift that has richly blessed them—and kept them young! See www.DannaDemetre.com.

LINDA DILLOW and her husband, Jody, lived in Europe and Asia for eighteen years as missionaries ministering in closed countries. Linda's new book, *What's It Like to Be Married to Me?* asks wives the same dangerous questions that Linda asks herself: "What is it like to make love with me?" "Why do I want to stay mad at you?" Linda is the author of the bestselling *Calm My Anxious Heart* and coauthor of *Intimate Issues*. A mother of four grown children and ten grandchildren, Linda now lives in Monument, Colorado. Go to www.intimateissues.com.

HARMONY DUST is the founder and executive director of Treasures, a Los Angeles–based nonprofit organization (outreach and support group) for women in the sex industry. Having overcome sexual abuse, rape, dysfunctional relationships, and a life inside the walls of a strip club working as an exotic dancer, Harmony is passionate about seeing women's hearts and lives revolutionized by a relationship with God. She also has a passion for seeing the house of God be a place where hurting and broken people are met with open arms. She has been featured in various media sources, including *Glamour.* She is a sought-after speaker and the author of *Scars & Stilettos.* See www.IAmATreasure.com and www.ScarsAndStilettos.com.

STASI ELDREDGE loves writing and speaking to women about the goodness of God. After graduating from San Diego State University with a bachelor's in sociology, Stasi joined Youth for Christ, heading up a ministry to pregnant teenagers and teen mothers. She has been active in ministry ever since, including theater ministry, crisis pregnancy center, and working with women's and children's ministry. She and her family live in Colorado. For more information, visit www.ransomedheart.com.

SHANNON ETHRIDGE is a bestselling author, international speaker, and certified life coach. She is the author of eighteen books, including the million-copy bestselling Every Woman's Battle series, the five-book Completely His series, and her latest book for the mainstream market, *The Sexually Confident Wife.* She is a frequent guest on television and radio programs. Shannon is most passionate about her role as a wife and best friend to her husband, Greg, and a mother and cheerleader to Erin and Matthew. Go to www.shannonethridge.com.

ANDREA FABRY is a former host of *Midday Connection* as well as a former journalist. She and her husband, Chris, are the parents of nine children ranging from young adult to school age. They reside in Vail, Arizona, where Andrea pursues her passion for health, nutrition, and environmental issues. She is the founder of Moms Against Mold. Visit Andrea's blog and website: www.moldrecovery.blogspot.com and www.momsagainstmold.org.

PAM FARREL with her husband, Bill, are international speakers, and authors of over thirty books including the bestselling *Men Are Like Waffles, Women Are Like Spaghetti.* She is a sought-after women's speaker and is the founder and president of Seasoned Sisters, a ministry to women 40–65 (www.seasonedsisters.com). Bill and Pam live in San Diego, have been happily married for thirty years, and are parents to three children, a daughter-in-law, and two small granddaughters. For more information, please visit www.billandpam.org.

MARGARET FEINBERG (www.margaretfeinberg.com) is a popular speaker and author of *Scouting the Divine, The Sacred Echo,* and

The Organic God, and their corresponding Bible studies. She can be reached at margaret@margaretfeinberg.com. Friend her on Facebook or follow her on Twitter @mafeinberg.

CHERI FULLER is a popular inspirational speaker and award-winning author of forty-two books including her newest, *Mother-Daughter Duet: Getting to the Relationship You Want with Your Adult Daughter* and *The One Year Women's Friendship Devotional.* A former Oklahoma Mother of the Year, Cheri speaks at women's retreats and conferences. She has been a frequent guest on *Focus on the Family* and other national radio and TV programs, and her articles have appeared in numerous publications. She and her husband, Holmes, have three grown children and live in Oklahoma. Visit www. cherifuller.com, which includes a blog, articles, free Bible studies, and other resources.

JILL RIGBY GARNER is a popular national speaker and award-winning author of *Raising Respectful Children in a Disrespectful World.* She founded Manners of the Heart as a nonprofit, using manners to teach respect for others. Jill speaks to thousands of parents, students, educators, and businesses each year. She shares her personal story of victory after loss with women of all ages offering hope in the midst of brokenness. She is also the host of the radio feature *Manners in a Minute,* and has been a guest on numerous television and radio programs. Evenings at home are spent with husband, Nick, God's sweetest blessing. Visit www.mannersoftheheart.org.

SANDRA GLAHN teaches at Dallas Theological Seminary, her alma mater, where she serves as editor in chief of *Kindred Spirit* magazine. Her books include *Mocha on the Mount, Espresso with Esther*, and many others in the Coffee Cup Bible Study series. She also is the author of *Informed Consent*, a medical suspense novel, and coauthor of numerous fiction and nonfiction works. Sandra leads retreats, seminars, and workshops on a variety of topics. She and Gary have been married for over thirty years and have one daughter, who joined their family through adoption. Visit www.aspire2. com.

Before **SARA GROVES** debuted in 1998, she was a high school teacher in her hometown of Rosemont, Minnesota. Through God's directing and leading, Sara left that job to pursue what had been a joy and a passion of hers since she was a little child. Sara is very involved with International Justice Mission, a team of lawyers and law enforcement officials who help women who are trapped in human trafficking. Her husband, Troy, is her manager and percussionist. Sara and Troy have three children: Kirby,

Toby, and Ruby. To learn more about Sara, please visit her website: www.
saragroves.com.

JANELLE HALLMAN is a licensed professional counselor in Denver. She
is also a popular international speaker on female homosexuality, human
brokenness, redemption, and healing. Her passion is to share God's Word
in a way that speaks to some of the deepest needs of broken and hurting
people. She has also been an adjunct professor at Colorado Christian University and Denver Seminary and is the executive director of Desert Hope
Ministries. Janelle completed her master's degree in counseling with hon-
ors at Denver Theological Seminary, is married, and has one daughter.
Visit www.janellehallman.com.

BECKY HARLING's life experience as a pastor's wife, mother of four,
women's ministry director, survivor of breast cancer, and childhood sexual abuse all bring depth and realism to her message. Becky speaks at
conferences, retreats, and other events both nationally and internationally, and has been a featured guest on television and radio programs. She
is the author of *Finding Calm in Life's Chaos, Rewriting Your Emotional
Script,* and *Freedom from Performing.* She and her husband, Steve, make
their church home at Foothills Community in Arvada, Colorado, where
Steve serves as the lead pastor. Together they are the parents of four
adult children and two grandchildren. Visit www.beckyharling.com.

LISA HARPER served for six years as the director of Focus on the Family's national women's ministry, followed by six years as the women's
ministry director at a large church, and she has earned a master's of theological studies from Covenant Seminary. Now a sought-after Bible
teacher and speaker, Lisa is currently featured on the national Women of
Faith tour and speaks at many other conferences. She's written nine
books, including *A Perfect Mess: Why You Don't Have to Worry about Being
Good Enough for God.* Visit www.lisaharper.net.

JOANNE HEIM is a wife, mom, teacher, and the author of several books,
including *Living Simply* and *Misplacing God: And Finding Him Again.* She
and her husband are also the authors of *Happily Ever After.* Joanne and
her family live in Denver, where she homeschools her daughters and is
working on her master's degree in Old Testament biblical studies at Denver Seminary. For more information, visit www.thesimplewife.typepad.
com.

DR. LAURA HENDRICKSON, a trained psychiatrist and biblical counselor, is the author of *Finding Your Child's Way on the Autism Spectrum:*

Discovering Unique Strengths, Mastering Behavior Challenges, coauthor of *Will Medicine Stop the Pain? Finding God's Healing for Depression, Anxiety, and Other Troubling Emotions,* and *When Good Kids Make Bad Choices: Help and Hope for Hurting Parents.* Laura is also a contributing author for *Women Counseling Women*, and two counseling anthologies. Visit www.drlaurahendrickson.com.

SHARON HERSH is a licensed professional counselor, author, and speaker. Her most recent book is *Begin Again, Believe Again: Sustaining the Courage to Love with Abandon.* She is also the author of *Bravehearts* and *The Last Addiction*, as well as four parenting books in the Hand-in-Hand parenting series. Sharon is an adjunct professor in counseling classes at several seminaries and a popular speaker at retreats and conferences. She lives in Lone Tree, Colorado, and can be contacted through www. sharonhersh.com or on Facebook.

BEV HISLOP is the associate professor of pastoral care to women at Western Seminary in Portland, Oregon. She is also the executive director of the Women's Center for Ministry, a global hub for training, resources, and networking for women in ministry. Bev and her colleagues have authored *Shepherding Women in Pain.* She also authored *Shepherding a Woman's Heart* and was a major contributing author to *Women's Ministry Handbook.* Bev earned a doctor of ministry degree from Gordon-Conwell Theological Seminary. Bev and Jim have two adult children and six living grandchildren. Jim is lead pastor at a church in Clackamas, Oregon.

MARILYN HONTZ speaks at conferences and retreats around the country about prayer and has been a featured guest on *Midday Connection* and *Focus on the Family.* She is the author of *Shamelifter* and *Listening for God.* She and her husband, Paul, head pastor of the 3,500-member Central Wesleyan Church in Holland, Michigan, have five children. Visit her blog at http://shamelifter.blogspot.com.

LYNNE HYBELS and her husband, Bill, started Willow Creek Community Church in suburban Chicago. She collaborated with the Willow Creek Association to develop Hope and Action—a DVD and participant's guide that helps churches and small groups begin to address the AIDS pandemic. She has authored *Nice Girls Don't Change the World.* She has traveled extensively in Africa and the Middle East. Lynne and Bill have two adult children and a grandson, Henry. Visitwww.lynnehybels.com.

JULIE-ALLYSON IERON is celebrating twenty-five years as an author, writing coach, editor, and conference speaker. The Julie-Allyson Ieron

Bible Reference Collection on WORDsearch 9.0. features nine of her books linked with seventy-five Bible reference resources. Additionally, most of her books are now available in MP3 audio and e-book, as well as print. Julie is a speaker and a frequent guest on radio and television broadcasts. Her book *The Overwhelmed Woman's Guide to . . . Caring for Aging Parents* has been a featured resource for Focus on the Family. She is a mentor/master craftsman with the Jerry B. Jenkins Christian Writer's Guild. Visit www.joymediaservices. com and http://womencareforagingparents. blogspot.com.

CAROLYN CUSTIS JAMES is a popular speaker for women's conferences, churches, colleges, seminaries, and other Christian organizations. Her ministry organization, WhitbyForum, promotes thoughtful biblical discussion to help men and women as they endeavor to extend God's kingdom together in a messy and complicated world. Carolyn founded and is president of a national organization for women emerging or engaged in ministry leadership. She has written several books, the latest being *Half the Church: Recapturing God's Global Vision for Women*. She and her husband live in Boxford, Massachusetts, and have one grown daughter. Visit www.whitbyforum.com and www.synergytoday.org.

DAWN HERZOG JEWELL is the author of *Escaping the Devil's Bedroom: Sex Trafficking, Global Prostitution and the Gospel's Transforming Power.* She loves writing and speaking about the global church and equipping others to reach the nations for Christ. Dawn has an MA in intercultural studies from Wheaton College Graduate School and has previously worked for the Billy Graham Center at Wheaton College and World Relief. She and her husband and son live in the Chicago suburbs. Visit www. escapingthedevilsbedroom.com.

VICTORIA SAUNDERS JOHNSON's desire is to inspire and teach women to study the Bible. She is a writer, speaker, and social worker based in Milwaukee. Victoria started Protecting Innocent Children, Inc., an initiative that is committed to helping and offering the hope of Christ to children and their families affected by childhood sexual abuse. She is the author of *Restoring Broken Vessels* and other works, and is the mother of three daughters.

NANCY KANE is an author, consultant, and a licensed clinical professional counselor, and currently serves as an associate professor of the precounseling major at Moody Bible Institute in Chicago. She and her husband, Ray, coauthored *From Fear to Love—Overcoming Barriers to*

Healthy Relationships. She has also written for *Counseling Today Journal* and is a contributing editor to the *Family Foundations Study Bible.* Nancy is a conference speaker who addresses a wide variety of topics. She and Ray have been married for over thirty years and have two adult children. www. moody.edu /edu_FacultyProfile.aspx?id=4512.

ELLIE KAY, "America's Family Financial Expert®," is a regular on *ABC NEWS Good Money* and a frequent guest on several radio and television outlets. She's a popular international speaker, a bestselling author, and a corporate educator who works with Fortune 100 companies. She says: "My profession is finances, but my passion is military families." To that end, she has spoken to over 500,000 military members and their families in the worldwide "Heroes at Home" tour, ministering hope and healing to the American military. She and her husband, Bob, a corporate test pilot, are the parents of seven children and live in Southern California. Visit www.elliekay.com.

CAROL KENT is a popular international public speaker best known for being dynamic, humorous, encouraging, and biblical. She is the president of Speak Up Speaker Services, a Christian speakers bureau, and the founder and director of Speak Up With Confidence seminars, a ministry committed to helping Christians develop their communication skills. She has recently founded the nonprofit organization Speak Up for Hope, which will benefit the families of incarcerated individuals. Carol's books include *When I Lay My Isaac Down, Speak Up with Confidence*, and *Becoming a Woman of Influence*. Visit www.carolkent.org.

GINGER KOLBABA is founding editor of Kyria.com and manager of discipleship resources for Christianity Today International. Also an accomplished author, Ginger has written more than 300 articles and has written or contributed to more than eighteen books, including the bestseller *Refined by Fire*. She's been quoted in national print media and has appeared on numerous radio and television programs. A graduate of Anderson University, Ginger worked as a professional actress and singer before making the transition to more sane and solitary roles behind a computer. Go to www.GingerKolbaba.com and www.Kyria.com.

BARBARA SHAW LARIMORE, also known as Barb, Mom, and Honey, hails from the deep South but calls Monument, Colorado, home for now. She is best known as the woman who carries a big stick and keeps Walt Larimore, MD, her husband of over thirty-five years, in line and walking the straight and narrow path! She is coauthor of the bestselling *His Brain, Her*

Brain, and speaks occasionally on the topic. You can learn more about Barb at www.DrWalt.com.

SUSIE LARSON is an author, national speaker, media voice for Moody Radio, and the host of the daily radio talk show *Live the Promise with Susie Larson*. Susie has written six books and a devotional journal, contributed to several books, published numerous articles, and writes a weekly blog. She and Kevin have been married for over twenty-five years and have three grown sons. She has been a guest on many radio programs. For more, visit www.susielarson.com.

HELEN LEE has been a writer and journalist in the Christian publishing market for more than fifteen years. She is the author *The Missional Mom* and served as coeditor and contributor of *Growing Healthy Asian-American Churches.* Helen has written numerous published articles, and in 2008 and 2009, won awards in reporting from the Evangelical Press Association for her articles "Five Kinds of Christians" and "Missional Shift or Drift?" that appeared in *Leadership Journal.* Helen and her husband, Brian, have three sons. Visit www.helenlee.info and www.themissionalmom.com.

ANITA LUSTREA is on a mission to communicate freedom to women. Her first book, *What Women Tell Me: Finding Freedom from the Secrets We Keep*, is her personal story woven in with the stories of women she's heard from through her years hosting *Midday Connection.* She has been the general editor and writer of *Daily Seeds from Women Who Walk in Faith, Come to Our Table*, and *Tending the Soul.* Anita and her husband, Mike, live in the Chicago area. Find Anita at www.anitalustrea.com, www.middayconnection.org, on Facebook, or Twitter @anitalustrea.

MARGARET MANNING earned her bachelor's degree in psychology from Agnes Scott College in Decatur, Georgia, before going on to earn her master of divinity degree from Gordon-Conwell Theological Seminary. Prior to working at Ravi Zacharias International Ministries as part of the writing and speaking team, Margaret served in pastoral roles focusing on teaching, discipleship, spiritual formation, and pastoral care and counseling. She and her husband, Sonny, reside in Seattle, Washington. For more information, go to: www.rzim.org.

CHRISTA MARCH is the wife of Jim and the mother to TJ and Loran. Since 1989 she has sought to demonstrate the love of Jesus Christ to teen mothers and their children first through the ministry of Teen Mother Choices and most recently through Teen Mother Choices International. If she were to have a life's motto, it would be *Coram Deo*, which means to live one's entire life in the presence of God, under the authority of God, to the glory of God. For more information, please visit: www.tmcint.org.

JENNIFER MARSHALL speaks and writes frequently on cultural issues as director of domestic policy studies at the Heritage Foundation, a Washington, DC–based think tank. She is a graduate of Wheaton College in Wheaton, Illinois, and of the Institute of World Politics in Washington, DC.

LEIGH MCLEROY has been a ghostwriter with seven books to her credit. Her first solo effort, *Moments for Singles*, was published by NavPress in 2004. She is the author of *The Beautiful Ache* and *The Sacred Ordinary*, and a contributor to *Daily Seeds*, a compilation devotional with *Midday Connection*. A frequent conference and event speaker, Leigh makes her home in Houston, Texas. To learn more about Leigh, please visit her website: www.leighmcleroy.com.

NANCY SEBASTIAN MEYER is a speaker and writer whose passion is to motivate women to renew their minds and adjust their actions. Her music brings renewed joy and comfort to listeners' hearts. Keynote speaker at Wives Only Workshop events, Nancy passes on the principles that rekindled her love for Rich, a pastor-turned-agnostic who gives her permission to share their story. Nancy and Rich live in an "empty nest" in Lancaster, Pennsylvania. For more information, please visit Nancy's website, www.hope4hearts.net.

JOANNE FAIRCHILD MILLER is a writer, artist, and speaker who enjoys taking an active part in the lives of her three married children and nine grandchildren. She is a volunteer at the Tennessee Prison for Women and a member of the Prism Art League. Joanne has authored two children's books based on the unique personalities of small children, *I Wanna Be ME* and *When I Am Quiet*. She and her husband, Dan, a bestselling author and career coach, speak at writers' conferences. Visit Joanne at www.48Days.com and www.48Days.net/profile/JoanneMiller.

SHAYNE MOORE is an outspoken advocate in the fight against extreme poverty and global AIDS. She is one of the original members of the ONE Campaign, the Campaign to Make Poverty History (www.one.org), and sits on the executive board of directors for Upendo Village, an HIV/AIDS clinic in Kenya. She was chosen to attend the G8 Summit as a delegate to both Gleneagles, Scotland, in 2005, and to St. Petersburg, Russia, in 2006, to urge world leaders to keep their promises to Africa and fully fund AIDS initiatives. Shayne lives in Illinois with her husband, John, and their three children. She blogs at http://theologymama.blogspot.com.

JENA MORROW shares her testimony of her recovery from anorexia nervosa in *Hollow: An Unpolished Tale*. She travels around the US sharing her recovery story and delivering a message of hope and freedom from disordered eating and distorted self-image, made possible through the abundant life Christ offers to those who follow Him. Jena also works as a behavioral health specialist in a residential treatment center for women struggling with eating disorders and other addictive illnesses. Jena and her son, Jaden, live in suburban Chicago. Visit www.jenamorrow.com or become a fan of "Hollow the Book" on Facebook.

LORI NEFF is the senior producer of *Midday Connection*. She grew up in a small town in Ohio, spending more time outside in nature than inside and is a graduate of Moody Bible Institute. Lori has been general editor and writer for three books: *Come to Our Table, Daily Seeds,* and *Tending the Soul*. Her interests include art (looking at it and creating it), music, literature, humanitarian aid efforts, camping, journaling, and spending time with her husband, John. Visit www.lorineff.com.

MIRIAM NEFF is the founder and president of Widowconnection.com. She is the author of nine books, the most recent being *From One Widow to Another: Conversations about the New You*. She hosts *New Beginnings*, a feature heard on over a thousand media outlets, and oversees projects for widows in Africa. The widow of Bob Neff, vice president of Moody Broadcasting, she delights in their four children and three grandchildren. For more information, please visit www.widowconnection.com.

LAURA PETHERBRIDGE is an international author and speaker who serves couples and single adults with topics on spiritual growth, relationships, coparenting, stepfamilies, divorce prevention, and divorce recovery. She is the author of *When "I Do" Becomes "I Don't"— Practical Steps for Healing during Separation and Divorce,* and *The Smart Stepmom* coauthored with Ron Deal. She has been a guest on numerous television and radio broadcasts, and, in addition to her books has written for many publications. Laura and her husband, Steve, reside in Florida. She is a stepmom of twenty-five years. Visit www.laurapetherbridge.com and www.TheSmartStepmom.com.

LORRAINE PINTUS: Rarely are the terms "godly saint" and "hormonally wacked-out woman" used to describe the same person except in Lorraine Pintus's book *Jump Off the Hormone Swing*, in which she explores what no one else talks about—the spiritual symptoms of PMS and perimenopause. Lorraine is an international speaker and bestselling author of three books with her friend Linda Dillow on God's perspective of sex: *Intimate Issues, Intimacy Ignited*, and *Gift-wrapped by God*, and has been a popular guest on TV and radio programs. Visit www.intimateissues.com and www.lorrainepintus.com.

DR. KARYN PURVIS is the founding director of the Institute of Child Development at Texas Christian University, whose focus for the past decade has been the development of interventions for at-risk children and their families. She is the coauthor of a bestselling adoption book titled *The Connected Child.* Karyn works tirelessly as an advocate for vulnerable children, testifying in court as well as working for legislation. Karyn is the mother of three grown sons and grandmother of eight precious children. Go to www.empoweredtoconnect.org.

You can find **MARTY RAMEY** hiking mountains almost every day, rain or shine. In nature, she finds inspiration for thought-provoking devotions and discussion-starters on which she collaborates for Trailbound Trips. She is equally passionate about serving others, especially the elderly. Marty currently works for a small family-owned insurance agency and is collaborating with Carol Ruhter on a book of outdoor devotions. She and her husband live in Maryland and have two adult sons who bring them immeasurable joy. Visit: www.TrailboundTrips.com.

MARCIA RAMSLAND is well known as "The Organizing Pro" for her practical skills to manage busy lives. Her tips appear in *Better Homes and Gardens, Real Simple* magazine, and on Martha Stewart radio. Marcia is the author of several popular books, including *Simplify Your Life, Simplify Your Time, Simplify Your Space, Simplify Your Holidays*, and *Ages and Stages of Getting Children Organized.* The newest product is a book and Bible study DVD series, *Simplify Your Life: 7 Weeks to a New You!* Visit www.organizingpro.com to get organized and stay that way!

CARYN DAHLSTRAND RIVADENEIRA is a popular writer and speaker. Her first book is the critically acclaimed *Mama's Got a Fake I.D.: How to Reveal the Real You behind All That Mom.* She is managing editor for the CTI's Gifted For Leadership blog and blogs at the Mommy Revolution, a site she cofounded. Caryn is also a regular contributor to CTI's Kyria.com and Her.Meneutics blog as well as Elisa Morgan's FulFill blog. Caryn's written dozens of magazine articles and lives in suburban Chicago with her husband, Rafael, and their three children. Visit Caryn at www.carynrivadeneira. com. Friend her Facebook at www.facebook.com/caryn.rivadeneira. Follow her on Twitter @CarynRivadeneira.

JANE RUBIETTA speaks internationally and is the critically acclaimed author of eleven books, including *Come Along: Journey to a More Intimate Faith*, and *Come Closer: A Call to Life, Love, and Breakfast on the Beach.* One airline captain told her, "Your books seem perfect for hurting women." She answered, "I've never met a woman who wasn't hurting." Her humor, vulnerability, and depth remind people they are not alone, and invite them into new places spiritually and emotionally. See www. JaneRubietta.com.

CAROL RUHTER is passionate about helping women rediscover intimacy with God by spending time outdoors, learning about the Creator through His creation. Her company, Trailbound Trips, offers women's hiking and biking trips and retreats. Carol is also a freelance writer and has been published in Midday's 2008 book, *Daily Seeds: From Women Who Walk In Faith* and in *Pearl Girls: Encountering Grit, Experiencing Grace.* She and her husband, Don, live in Barrington, Illinois, and have two adult children.

JILL SAVAGE is the founder and CEO of Hearts at Home, a ministry for moms. The author of seven books, including *Real Moms . . . Real Jesus, My Hearts at Home*, and *Living with Less So Your Family Has More,* Jill is a sought-after speaker known for her humor and honesty. Jill and her husband, Mark, have five children and live in Normal, Illinois. You can find Jill online at www.jillsavage.org and www.hearts-at-home.org.

MARLO SCHALESKY is the award-winning author of several books, including *Shades of Morning*, which combines a love story with a surprise ending twist to create a new type of novel that she hopes will touch readers at their deepest levels. Marlo's other books include the Christy Award–winning novel *Beyond the Night*, as well as her nonfiction *Empty Womb, Aching Heart: Hope and Help for Those Struggling with Infertility.* Marlo has earned her master's in theology, with an emphasis in biblical studies, from Fuller Theological Seminary. Marlo lives with her husband and five young children in a log home in central California. Visit www. VividGod.com.

MELINDA SCHMIDT grew up in Wheaton, Illinois, listening to Moody Radio's flagship station, WMBI FM. A career in broadcasting appears to have been inevitable! As a kid, she was eager to grab the mic of the family's Wallensak tape machine to record make-believe news broadcasts and imaginary radio shows. Early "broadcasts" have her announcing the arrival of "the Beagles"—otherwise known as "the Beatles"—to America. Melinda is a graduate of Moody Bible Institute and holds a BS in Broadcasting-Bible from Calvary Bible College. She and her husband, Dave, are the parents of two young adults. Visit www.melindaschmidt.com.

MONA SHRIVER worked as an emergency room nurse until the Lord called her out of that profession and into ministry. She is a Precept-trained Bible teacher, has been active in women's ministries, and speaks at special events and retreats. She serves her local church body in central California. She and her husband, Gary, cofounded Hope & Healing Ministries Inc., which provides support and resources for couples in adultery recovery. Mona has written for several publications, and she and Gary have been guests on numerous radio and television programs. They have three grown sons.

JAN SILVIOUS has been reaching out to women for over twenty years, helping them to think biblically, reason clearly, live fully, and embrace an intelligent attitude toward life. As a featured speaker at numerous events and conferences across the country, Jan has encouraged audiences across the country and across every denomination, challenging them to grow into the women God has called them to be. She has been featured on numerous television and radio programs. She is the author of ten books, including *Big Girls Don't Whine* and *Fool-Proofing Your Life*. Visit www.jansilvious.com.

DR. JULIANNA SLATTERY is a Christian psychologist, speaker, wife, and mother. She serves as family psychologist at Focus on the Family and as an adjunct professor of marriage and family studies with the Focus Leadership Institute, and is the author of *No More Headaches: Enjoying Sex and Intimacy in Marriage*, and other titles. Juli has been a featured speaker at churches and on nationwide radio, including *Midday Connection*. She is a regular contributor to Focus on the Family broadcasting and publications. Juli and her husband, Mike, live in Colorado Springs, and are the parents of three boys.

KENDRA SMILEY is a sought-after speaker, an author, and the host of *Live Life Intentionally*, heard nationally on Moody Radio. An Illinois Mother of the Year, Kendra and her husband, John, have three married sons and four granddaughters. She and John, a retired USAF Colonel, live on a farm in central Illinois. Together they have written the www.ParentinglikeaPro.com book series. Kendra's passions include parenting, women's issues, and education. For more information, go to Kendra's website: www.KendraSmiley.com.

An award-winning writer, **ANN SPANGLER** is the author of many best-selling books, including *Women of the Bible* (coauthored with Jean Syswerda), *Praying the Names of God, Praying the Names of Jesus,* and *Sitting at the Feet of Rabbi Jesus* (coauthored with Lois Tverberg). Together, her books have sold nearly three million copies. She lives with her two daughters in Grand Rapids, Michigan. For more information, please visit http://annspangler.com/.

In 1992, **ARLOA SUTTER** opened an unused church storefront room and began to serve hot coffee and lunch to the homeless. Today, Breakthrough stands as a center of hope for the community residents and families of Chicago's West side. Arloa is a graduate of Moody Bible Institute and holds a doctorate of ministry degree from the Bakke Graduate University and an MA in urban missions from Lincoln Christian University. She serves on the staff of the River City Community Church and on the boards of the Christian Community Development Association and the Chicago Low-Income Housing Trust Fund. Visit www.breakthrough.org.

BEVERLY HUBBLE TAUKE, LCSW, is a speaker and author serving among a group of Virginia Christian family counselors. She has facilitated workshops for homeless men and women, taught journalism and communications at a Christian college in Kenya, and managed media relations in the US House and Senate. The author of *Healing Your Family Tree*, Bev has also written articles for both Christian and mainstream publications. She holds graduate degrees from Wheaton College and the Catholic University of America. Beverly and her husband, Tom, have two young adult children.

ANGELA THOMAS is a bestselling author and speaker who has been teaching the Bible for over twenty-five years. She is a graduate of the University of North Carolina and Dallas Theological Seminary. Angela and her family live in North Carolina. For more information, please visit Angela's website: www.angelathomas.com.

Author and speaker **JANET THOMPSON** is the founder of Woman to Woman Mentoring and About His Work Ministries. Sharing life's experiences and God's faithfulness is the premise of Janet's books and speaking. She is the author of *The Team That Jesus Built, Face-to-Face Bible Study Series, Praying for Your Prodigal Daughter, Dear God, They Say It's Cancer*, and Woman to Woman Mentoring Resources. For more information, go to Janet's website: www.womantowomanmentoring.com.

SIBYL TOWNER is the coauthor of *Listen to My Life* and cofounder of oneLifeMaps.com, an organization dedicated to helping people review their life stories for the purpose of recognizing and responding to God. Currently, she serves in various aspects of ministry within Willow Creek Church and is part of the faculty for Classes@Willow. A frequent speaker and workshop leader, she has also taught internationally in the area of spiritual formation. She has completed four years of instructional experience in Spiritual Leadership with the Transforming Center. Sibyl and her husband currently reside in a suburb of Chicago.

DONNA VANLIERE is the *New York Times* and *USA Today* bestselling author of *The Christmas Shoes, The Angels of Morgan Hill*, and *Finding Grace*. She lives in Tennessee with her husband and three children. Visit Donna at www.donnavanliere.com.

LESLIE VERNICK is a popular speaker, author, licensed clinical social worker, and life coach with a private counseling practice in Pennsylvania. She is the author of six books, including the bestselling, *The Emotionally Destructive Relationship* and her most recent, *Lord, I Just Want to Be Happy*. Leslie currently serves on the Board of Directors for Lighthouse Network, a Christian mental health outreach ministry and Beneath His Wings, a Christian outreach for women needing shelter from abusive relationships. Leslie and her husband, Howard, have been married for over thirty years, have two adult children, and love being new grandparents. Visit www.leslievernick.com.

CINDY WEST is an international consultant and speaker who works alongside those who desire to release artists for the ministry to which God has called them. She is also an artist who has created recognized art in several mediums—photography, fiber arts, paint, and video. In addition, Cindy has recently founded Awakening Artists, an international ministry committed to creating missional art that displays both beauty and brokenness in our world. Today, she lives in the foothills of the Rockies. Go to www.awakeningartists.com.

ANGIE WESZELY is dedicated to offering holistic, innovative solutions to the issue of abortion by mobilizing Christians to work for the dignity and welfare of both the woman and the child. As president of Caris, a Christian pregnancy counseling agency, Angie supports women facing unplanned pregnancy in ways that reflect God's heart. She and her husband have a teenage daughter and a preschool son, so she knows firsthand the challenges of balancing family with career. Visit www.supportgrace.org and www.caris.org.

SANDRA WILSON is an author, seminary professor, counseling consultant, and international speaker who served on the executive board of the AACC. She is currently a spiritual director. Sandra and her family live in Tennessee.

VINITA HAMPTON WRIGHT is a novelist, editor, workshop facilitator, and freelance writer. Go to her Book List to read about her novels and nonfiction books. Her most recent, *Days of Deepening Friendship*, explores the spirituality of women's experience. She conducts workshops on creativity and spirituality across the country as well as regular online retreats. You can stay up-to-date with her events and writing life by checking out her information at vinitawright.typepad.com.

CHRISTINE WYRTZEN is the founder and director of Daughters of Promise, a unique ministry for women. She is also a recording artist, author, inspirational speaker, creative Bible teacher, storyteller, and host of the daily, nationally syndicated radio program *Daughters of Promise.* Her success in helping women discover the heart of God is due to her warmth and transparency, and her own rebirth in 1997. She has been married for over thirty-five years to Ron Wyrtzen, youngest son of the evangelist, Jack Wyrtzen, and they have two adult children and two grandsons. See www.daughtersofpromise.org and www.christinewyrtzen.com.

KAY YERKOVICH is a licensed therapist with a master's degree in counseling. She has been using attachment theory in her professional counseling of couples and families for more than fifteen years. Kay and her husband, Milan, speak internationally on the book they coauthored, *How We Love.* The Yerkovichs experienced an awakening to deeper intimacy and emotional connection fifteen years into their own marriage when they discovered the powerful connection between the past and its influence on the present through the principles of attachment theory. The couple's second book, *How We Love Our Kids,* looks at the impact different love styles have on parenting. See www.howwelove.com.

All websites and phone numbers listed herein are accurate at the time of publication but may change in the future or cease to exist. The listing of website references and resources does not imply publisher endorsement of the site's entire contents. Groups and organizations are listed for informational purposes, and listing does not imply publisher endorsement of their activities.

DAILY SEEDS

ISBN-13: 978-0-8024-7561-9

Scripture encourages us to be immersed in the Word of God. In this book, women will be enlightened by the wisdom and wit of authors and speakers such as Lisa Whelchel, Mary Hunt, Dee Brestin, Priscilla Shirer, Dannah Gresh, and more than 50 others. Includes reflective questions.

MOODY
PUBLISHERS

moodypublishers.com

COME TO OUR TABLE

ISBN-13: 978-1-881273-90-5

Filled with tasty appetizers to desserts from your favorite authors like Dannah Gresh, Nancy Leigh DeMoss, and Liz Curtis Higgs, as well as radio personalities across Moody Radio, *Come to Our Table* will be a collectible in and out of Moody Radio's listening audience.

MOODY
PUBLISHERS

moodypublishers.com

PEARL GIRLS

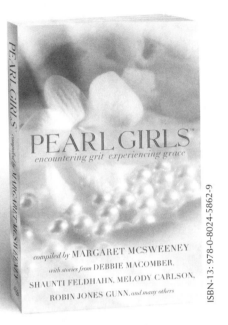

Perhaps you've heard the story of the oyster that gets a piece of sand stuck inside its shell. Nacre coats this irritant and creates a pearl. Like the oyster, we encounter unexpected grit in our lives; however, God's nacre of love and grace covers our pain and transforms us into precious pearls. Read these true stories about women who have encountered grit and experienced grace through the tough times life can throw at us.

MOODY
PUBLISHERS

moodypublishers.com